Business/Corporate Community

"How is it that certain people in times of such crises never waver or falter, but instead exhibit remarkable endurance and faithfulness in accomplishing one's mission? The answer is leadership that respects, dignifies, and serves others; leadership that stirs souls, heals hearts, touches lives. In these pages, Lee Ellis shares extraordinary stories of courage, resiliency, honor, and humility from which we can learn about such transformative leadership and apply these insights to today's workplace."

Michael Montelongo
SVP & Chief Administrative Officer,
On-site Service Solutions, Sodexo North America

"In *Leading with Honor*, Lee Ellis shows us that the principles of leadership he experienced during some of the most difficult situations as a POW are applicable to leaders everywhere. Lee's candid narrative is compelling, giving us an appreciation for the importance of leading with honor and courage, even in the face of the most difficult adversity."

Ralph de la Vega
President and CEO, AT&T Mobility and Consumer Markets,
Author of *Obstacles Welcome: Turn Adversity into Advantage in Business and Life*

"*Leading with Honor* brings forth the characteristics of leadership like no other. No matter how successful one may become, there are always internal questions about leadership. Lee's book not only strengthens my beliefs about leadership, it lifts my vision even higher through the examples of leaders under extreme circumstances. To me leadership under these extremes illustrates the epitome of 'great leadership.'"

Thomas (Tom) Crawford
CEO of Crawford Corporate Coaching;
Chairman of the National Organization, CEONetweavers;
past President and CEO at Prudential of America,
Crawford & Company, and Southern Heritage Insurance Company

"True leadership is that which surfaces when one is tested in the most severe of arenas. The leadership lessons Lee Ellis imparts in this compelling work come from just such an arena. Those lessons do much to inform all of us who lead in these challenging times."

John R. Lough, EdD
Manager, Professional Development Programs,
The BB&T Banking School, BB&T University

"As I read *Leading with Honor*, I thought, 'Imagine if ALL the leaders of our country—from the President, to the members of Congress, to our state government leaders were elected based upon their commitment to the standards and leadership qualities that Lee describes as hallmarks and guideposts for leading with honor'. How quickly the United States could re-assert its reputation not only as the envy of the world as a leading industrial nation, but as the brightest beacon of light and hope and honor on the planet."

Bob Littell
Chief NetWeaver, NetWeaving.com

"The book captures the true essence of successful leadership principles in a precise, succinct manner as translated from the actions of the brave heroes at the Hanoi Hilton. We as civilian executives need to return to these basic principles of honorable servant leadership more so than ever, given these turbulent times and a pervasive me-first short term thinking attitude that dominates our business and political cultures."

Darryl W. Jackson
Managing Director, KMJ Partners LLC,
Fortune 500 Senior Executive and Big 4 Partner

"*Leading with Honor* is an introspective read offering character and leadership parallels from prisoner of war (POW) camps to today's challenging business environment. Lee does a thought provoking, masterful job sharing his personal experiences in captivity and integrating those into principles for leadership success. This book is a must read, authored by a unique individual who continues to give back to those he so courageously served and protected – the leaders of today and tomorrow."

Ed Day
President and CEO, Mississippi Power Company

"It isn't often that you have a chance to read authentic leadership examples from real life. That is what Lee Ellis has provided through *Leading with Honor*. Lee gives us an inside glimpse at what makes true leaders great – selfless servanthood based on integrity and discipline. This is a book you just can't put down once you open the cover. Inside will well up a sense of pride in our country and those who serve as Lee takes us into the details of true leaders who bled red, white and blue!"

Arlin Sorenson
CEO of Heartland Technology Solutions,
Leader of Heartland Technology Groups

"Powerful and compelling, Lee Ellis does a masterful job of translating his experiences in captivity into thoughtful and thought-provoking leadership lessons applicable in all walks of life."

Susan A. McLaughlin,
President & CEO, VickPark Associates, LLC

Military Community

"In *Leading with Honor,* Lee uses gripping stories from the POW camps to engage the reader and teach invaluable principles of leadership. I highly recommend this book for developing leaders at all levels in any organization, military or civilian."

William R. Looney III, General USAF (Ret)

"A wonderful book! Leadership advice obtained and forged from the burning fire of captivity and adversity at the Hanoi Hilton. This book offers great wisdom and advice about leadership. The wisdom was earned with suffering, sadness and pain. I am pleased to recommend this book to you."

COL Jim Coy (Ret)
Author, The Eagles Series books *Prisoners of Hope – A Gathering of Eagles*

"I first met Lee Ellis in a North Vietnamese Prison. Leaders emerged of course, and Lee was among them. He seemed to understand, better than most, what was required to maintain harmony and cohesion in that naturally tense environment. Anyone seeking a better understanding of how to lead and manage others, in any kind of organization, will profit from this book."

General Charles G. Boyd, USAF (Ret)
Former President and CEO, Business Executives for National Security (BENS)
2002-2009; Center for the National Interest, Starr Distinguished Fellow for
National Security, Director at BENS, DRS Technologies, and I-Q-Tell;
Board of Visitors, Air University, USAF

"Lee Ellis has captured the essence of what leaders do and the guiding principles they use that place them ahead of the pack. He skillfully uses his experience as a five and half year POW during the Vietnam War. He tells what it takes to build an underground civilization with its laws, rules for survival, and a covert communication system. The leaders stepped forward and led 500 fellow POWS home with honor."

RADM R. Byron Fuller, USN (Ret)

"As a former POW, Lee's book is a truly outstanding explanation of what we witnessed, describing great examples, naming names and incidents that had such a spectacular effect on our morale and survival. I thank Lee from the bottom of my heart for doing such a great job in analyzing and conveying the message of what moral and effective leadership is all about."

Guy D. Gruters, USAF POW 12/1967 to 3/1973

"WOW! Col Lee Ellis has given us a true gift – real solutions to today's leadership issues against a backdrop of real human survival in Prisoner of War status. This wonderful book is a must read for all who aspire to any leadership job! An absolute 'page turner' and tribute to our warriors of a by-gone era, with lessons for today."

Lt Gen William Lord, USAF

"He clearly and artfully applies these lessons to contemporary leadership situations in an eminently practical and engaging manner. In short, there are thousands of leadership books and leadership 'experts,' but few can hope to approach the authenticity which Lee Ellis brings to *Leading with Honor*. Highly recommended for leaders of all ages and experience levels!"

Hon. John Scott Redd, Vice Admiral, U. S. Navy (Ret)
First Director of the National Counterterrorism Center,
Founding Commander of the U. S. Fifth Fleet

"A great read on integrity, character, and leadership. Those of us that shared the crucible of the 'Hanoi Hilton' learned much about ourselves, but more importantly, what God, country, and freedom really means. Lee captures the essence of what it takes to provide strong leadership, as well as followership, in some of the most difficult conditions ever faced by our military men."

R. E. "Gene" Smith
Past President and Chairman of the Board,
Air Force Association, Pow 25 Oct 67- 14 Mar 73

Healthcare Community

"Lee has captured many powerful lessons through his many years of experience in this gripping read. He has used those lessons with us as our team has evolved over the past several years. His leadership and facilitation have helped us to grow as leaders individually as well as become a strong team."

Carol Burrell
President and CEO, Northeast Georgia Health Systems

Non-Profit Community

"I have admired Lee Ellis for years. Lee has done a superb job of drawing from the deep well of his unforgettable experiences as a POW to bring us a refreshing cup of wisdom for life and leading. Our culture desperately needs to hear his inspiring story, and even more so these fourteen lessons on leading with honor. I whole-heartedly recommend it!"

Howard Dayton
Founder, Compass—Finances God's way

"Lee's remarkable journey and ability to take what would for most be considered a dark time, and turn it into an opportunity to teach leadership is a genuine gift. Transforming prison life experiences to leadership learning surpasses others attempt to write on leadership."

Bob Pedersen
Chief Visionary & Storyteller, Goodwill NCW

"Lee's painful and humorous stories touch deeply, reminding us of the sacrifices that POW leaders made to serve our nation with honor. From those dry bones, he brings life and light through case studies and stories from today's workplace, showing us how authentic leaders in every generation lean into the pain to do the right thing."

Laurie Beth Jones
Author, Jesus CEO and Jesus Life Coach

Academic Community

"In the crowded world of books on leadership, Lee Ellis's unique contribution, *Leading with Honor,* rises well above the standard fare on this topic. His book is so authentic in that he has personally experienced most of the lessons he promotes. This book far exceeds anything I've seen and its story telling style woven into strong, practical wisdom makes it hard to put down."

Archie B. Carroll
Director, Nonprofit Management & Community Service
Program and Professor of Management *Emeritus,*
Terry College of Business, University of Georgia

LEADING
with
HONOR

Leadership Lessons from the Hanoi Hilton

Lee Ellis

FreedomStar
Media

Published by FreedomStar Media

ISBN 9780983879305

Drawings from *Prisoner of War: Six years in Hanoi* by John M. McGrath, LCDR U.S. Navy, Copyright © 1975 U.S. Naval Institute, Annapolis, Maryland. Reprinted by Permission of Naval Institute Press

THE HOLY BIBLE, NEW INTERNATIONAL VERSION®, NIV® Copyright © 1973, 1978, 1984, 2011 by Biblica, Inc.™ Used by permission. All rights reserved worldwide.

Cover Design: Mighty 8th Media
Interior Art and Layout Design: Marshall Still - Still Graphics
Content Editor: Michael Dowling
Copy Editor: Valerie Dyke

Trade distribution is provided by the Greenleaf Book Group. To purchase this book for trade distribution, go to FreedomStarMedia.com / Media.

FreedomStar Media

Publisher's Cataloging-in-Publication data

Ellis, Lee, 1943 -
    Leading with honor : leadership lessons from the Hanoi Hilton / Lee Ellis.
    p. cm.
    Includes index.
    ISBN 9780983879305 (Hardcover)
1. Leadership. 2. Organizational effectiveness. 3. Teams in the workplace. 4. Character. 5. Courage.
6. Vietnam War, 1961-1975 --Influence. 7. Vietnam War, 1961-1975 --Prisoners and prisons, North Vietnamese. 8. Vietnam War, 1961-1975 --Personal narratives, American. 9. Prisoners of war --United States. 10. Prisoners of war --Vietnam. I. Title.

HD66 .E425 2011
658.4 / 02 –dd22   2011940340

Printed in the USA

18 19 20 21 22 23 – 10 9 8 7 6 5 4 3 2
8th Printing

TABLE OF CONTENTS

FOREWORD

Lee Ellis and I share a bond that goes back to our experience in the POW camps of North Vietnam. He was captured eleven days after me, and we occupied neighboring cells in the Hanoi Hilton for eighteen months of our captivity. When the peace agreements were signed, we paced the open compound at the Plantation Camp together, waiting for our release date. We have been friends ever since.

In *Leading with Honor* Lee draws from the POW experience, including some of his own personal story, to illustrate the crucial impact of leadership on the success of any organization. His writings highlight lessons and principles that can be applied to every leadership situation.

Lee also addresses the role of honor in leadership. Unfortunately, we don't hear much about honor in discussions of civilian leadership, but our businesses, governmental institutions, and charitable organizations desperately need to conduct that conversation. Leading with honor is about putting service to others ahead of self-interests. It means keeping your word and your commitments. It means serving sacrificially in a way that upholds the values that historically have made our nation great, our people proud, and our families strong.

My friend Lee Ellis presents these lessons in an exciting and practical way. *Leading with Honor* is a book that can have a positive influence on the development of every leader. I thank Lee for bringing this conversation to the forefront of our national discussion.

John McCain
United States Senator
POW 1967 - 1973

INTRODUCTION

Our culture desperately needs courageous servant leaders—men and women who have clear vision and strong character, who instill confidence and inspire excellence, who don't fold under pressure, compromise on principle, or practice deception. In short, we need leaders who are committed to *leading with honor*.

I had the privilege of serving under such exemplary leaders for sixty-four months, seven days a week, twenty-four hours a day. I had no choice about the long hours. We were locked up together as prisoners of war in the infamous "Hanoi Hilton" prison system.

The American leaders in the North Vietnamese POW camps were some of the most highly qualified and best trained officers we've ever sent to war. These men suffered torture and deprivation of the worst kind for six, seven, and even eight years, yet they courageously kept on leading.

When they were beaten down, they didn't conceal their shortcomings or wallow in self-pity. They picked themselves up and continued to lead with inspirational courage and unselfish devotion. There's nothing quite like the crucible of a POW camp for revealing authenticity. When you're enduring hunger and humiliation, punctuated by frequent threats of torture and even death, pretenses get stripped away fast. You are completely vulnerable; transparency is the only option. You come face-to-face with doubts and fears you never knew you had.

Although I'll tell you some of my story, a more important goal is to tell you about the leaders I saw in action. They are my heroes. I commend them to you as role models. We wholeheartedly followed these leaders because we respected and trusted them. They were brave, unselfish, and genuine.

In the Hanoi Hilton I learned that leading with honor is about doing the right thing, even when it entails personal sacrifice. More often than not, doing the right things—accepting responsibility, fulfilling your duty, telling the truth, and remaining faithful to your word—is the most difficult thing to do, but it's also the thing that brings long-term success. Shortcuts may work for the moment, but almost everything of lasting value comes at a price. For the POW leaders in the Hanoi system, that price was very high indeed.

I've made many speeches over the years since the war. Often people come up afterward and say, "I could never have done what you did." I sense that behind that comment they're really asking themselves, "Could I do that? Do I have what it takes to survive a POW experience with honor?"

In this book I pose a deeper and more helpful question: "Do you have what it takes to lead with honor where you are now—with your team, your family, your community, and your country?" I've written this book to help you answer that question, hopefully with a resounding yes! If you lead from a strong foundation, you will succeed in any battle that comes your way.

A POW camp—one of the most intense and stressful environments imaginable—provides an excellent vehicle for identifying and validating basic principles for leading with honor. The fourteen lessons that follow come from that crucible; they have been further refined through my lifelong focus on leadership.

Finding Leaders Worth Emulating

In times of tremendous challenges and tumultuous changes, one thing remains constant: the importance of the leader. Think about it. Who's responsible for building the culture of the organization? Who ultimately must attract the talent, communicate the vision, foster the teamwork, and set the standards? Who must provide the inspiration necessary for the organization to overcome obstacles, navigate through uncertainty, and accomplish the mission? The answer, of course, is the leader.

Leaders have another equally important responsibility: to develop new leaders. Effective leadership is typically *caught* more than *taught*.

That means successful leaders must serve as role models for aspiring leaders.

Unfortunately, some people did not have good leaders to emulate early in their careers, and most caught some poor habits along the way. Compelling stories about outstanding leaders can help fill the gap. From these stories we can gain freedom from the past and vision for the future. We can learn what it means to lead with honor, and we can develop the tools and the mindsets we need to do it.

In these pages I'll share accounts of leaders who served as my role models. As you read about them, I think you'll see why they had such a significant influence on me. And more importantly, I think you'll learn from them too.

Embarking On a Mission

Since being set free from captivity in North Vietnam, my evolving mission has been to help free leaders from the shackles that prevent them from becoming the best they can be. In my years as a leadership consultant, I have assessed, coached, and trained hundreds of men and women in myriad professions and levels of responsibility. They have included executives of Fortune 500 companies and top leaders in the health care industry, entrepreneurs and educators, politicians and physicians, and plant supervisors and pastors. Although most were already moderately to very successful, they were committed to continuous growth and development.

This book is for men and women who want to elevate their influence and effectiveness to the next level. Does that include you? Do you want to unleash more of your leadership potential? Would you like people to wholeheartedly follow you because you have earned their trust and respect, not simply because you have authority over them? Would you like your character to speak louder than your commands?

If your answer is yes, I have good news for you. To experience the power of leading with honor, you don't need to become a POW or endure a similar trial. Through honest self-assessment and the application of the principles outlined in this book, you can become a more successful leader. I know that to be true, because for many years I have personally grappled with and applied these principles, and I've helped others do the same.

Becoming a Warrior

But be forewarned: becoming a better leader is not easy. First, your ego will sting a bit when you realize that you have not arrived and still have room to grow. Second, changing some of your attitudes, behaviors, and habits can be difficult, even painful. In a very real sense, you must become a warrior. You must go to war with your ego, your dogmatic opinions, and some of your old ways of doing things—the practices that really don't work.

There is a price to pay if you want to lead with honor. One of the most famous epic dramas of our time—*The Lord of the Rings: The Return of the King*—describes the cost this way:

There is no freedom without sacrifice.
There is no victory without loss.
There is no glory without suffering.

What are you willing to sacrifice to gain your freedom from the hindrances that are holding you back? What are you willing to lose or give up to enjoy the victory of greater leadership success? I encourage you to put forth the effort and lean into the pain. Even a modest investment will yield big results.

Planning Your Flight

If you're ready to embark on this mission, allow me to give you our flight plan. The first part of this book is about leading yourself. My aim is to help you dig beneath the surface to gain a better understanding of what you value, where you want to go, and what you are willing to sacrifice to get there. We'll examine a few key concepts like self-knowledge, character, attitude, courage, determination, and resiliency.

The second part of the book is about leading others. That's where we talk about the vital leadership issues of organizational culture, communication, accountability, continuous growth, balancing mission and people, teamwork, innovation, and celebration.

In each chapter I'll use stories from the POW camps, including some of my personal experiences, as a springboard for highlighting leadership principles and examples. At the end of each chapter, I've provided personal coaching designed to help you apply these principles. If you would like to print out an expanded version of these coaching questions for your use in writing your responses, visit LeadingWithHonor.com.

In flight school when an instructor stomped a foot, or simply said, "This is a foot stomper," we knew we'd better pay attention, because what followed was likely to appear on the test. In this book I've included a "Foot Stomper" at the end of each chapter that summarizes that chapter's key point. It's intended to help you succeed on the leadership tests in your life.

Gaining Freedom

When I was released from captivity in North Vietnam, it was as though a great weight had been lifted from my shoulders. Now, as a consultant and coach, I have the joy and privilege of helping leaders throw off the weights of counterproductive behaviors and self-defeating mindsets, so they can lead with greater courage, conviction, purpose, and passion.

I hope this book will help you gain similar freedom, so you can, more than ever, *lead with honor*.

Lee Ellis

LEADING YOURSELF

Chapter 1

KNOW YOURSELF

★

"This above all: to thine ownself be true,
And it must follow, as the night the day,
Thou canst not then be false to any man."

William Shakespeare, Hamlet 1, iii

November 7, 1967, 4:00 p.m.—Captain Ken Fisher and I rolled into a dive-bomb pass in our F-4C Phantom jet. As we swooped downward, our bird with turned-up wingtips, elevated tail, and deafening roar must have resembled a high-tech version of a prehistoric pterodactyl.[1]

Tracers from the North Vietnamese antiaircraft artillery flashed by our canopy like giant Roman candles, their explosions encircling us with ominous puffs of gray and black smoke, each representing hundreds of shards of shrapnel designed to mortally wound our beautiful beast. It was combat as it has been for thousands of years, just updated with the latest technology.

Our mission was to destroy the guns that protected the Quang Khe ferry near Route 1A, the main thoroughfare for transporting war materials to the Ho Chi Minh Trail. As our jet plunged toward the artillery positions at five hundred miles an hour, the earth enlarged in our windscreen as if we were adjusting the zoom of a telephoto lens. It was an eyeball-to-eyeball stare-down with the enemy, with each side expecting the other to die. When you face enemy fire, you are at the point of the sword. Ken and I had been around long enough to know that the sword of combat cuts both ways; we had lost three close friends in similar situations in the prior two months.

We released our heavy payload of bombs, and our lightened plane lurched upward. Suddenly, an explosion rocked our aircraft. A terrifying sound, like marbles in a blender, alerted me that the metal of our expensive flying machine was ripping apart. The cockpit was still intact, but it was rapidly filling with smoke. The control stick was frozen full aft right, and we were tumbling end over end through the sky.

Just before bomb release we had been at six thousand feet, descending rapidly in a steep dive. Now, on fire and out of control, there was only one option: eject. But that was impossible! I was upside down floating out of my seat with my head pushed against the top of the canopy. If I ejected while we were in negative Gs[2], I could suffer severe injury, even death. But time was running out; at our rate of descent, we would soon be out of the envelope for safe ejection.

Suddenly the cockpit flipped again, and I felt pressure in my seat: positive Gs! It was now or never. I sat upright and pulled the ejection handle. An explosive charge fired, blowing away the canopy. Still strapped in my seat, I was blasted free of the aircraft—like a carnival stunt artist shot from a cannon—at an acceleration force eighteen times the force of gravity.[3]

Now, if this expensive, one-time-use Martin-Baker ejection system was going to save my life, it would have to flawlessly execute a remarkably complex series of events. A half-second later, the man-seat separator worked as advertised, firing a blast of compressed air to open the lap-belt connecting pin, freeing me from the heavy seat and triggering the appropriately named "butt snapper"—a folded nylon belt under my seat that mechanically snapped tight, thrusting me into space. As the ejection seat moved away, the attached lanyard pulled out the D-Ring, deploying my parachute. The F-4 Phantom's marvelously engineered James Bond-like escape system had snatched me from the jaws of death in less than two seconds.

But much like Bond's adventures, escape from one danger only brought another. I had ejected from the womb of the F-4 into a very unfriendly world. Hanging in the parachute without my shell of protection, I felt exposed and vulnerable. Gunfire cracked below and bullets whizzed by me. Instinctively, I followed the procedures ingrained by regular refresher training since entering flight school:

Check for a fully open chute. Activate the emergency beeper. Decide on deploying the life raft. Pick a spot to land and steer your parachute. Prepare for the parachute-landing fall (PLF).

To the west, the landscape was dotted with foliage-covered karsts, which rose like giant green cones several hundred feet into the air. Snaking among these majestic limestone formations, like a silver ribbon, flowed the Song Gianh River. To the east, the river broadened as it encountered the flat terrain of the delta, until it emptied into the azure waters of the Gulf of Tonkin, now shimmering in the late afternoon sun. This pastoral scene and the gentle sounds of the wind rustling through the canopy of my parachute for an instant made me forget my danger, but I was soon jarred back to reality by the crack of gunfire and the jabber of alien voices below.

Situational awareness dictated that my best opportunity to escape was to steer the chute to reach the river. We were only a couple of miles from the gulf. If I could make it to the river, there might be a chance of evading capture long enough to be picked up by a rescue boat or helicopter. I pulled on the risers and steered, but there was insufficient altitude to glide the distance. Fortunately, I was not far from the coast, so the terrain beneath my feet was relatively flat. Picking a spot about two hundred yards north of the river, I executed the PLF: boots hit the ground first; then roll to spread the energy of deceleration sequentially over legs, thighs, hips, shoulders, and upper back. No sprains, nothing broken—the sergeants had trained us well.

I scampered into a waist-deep bomb crater about ten feet from where I had landed, pulled the quick-release clamps to disconnect myself from the deflating parachute, and grabbed my radio: "This is Buckshot 2 Bravo. I'm on the ground, but they're closing in. Start strafing three hundred meters north of the river. I'm heading south." But help didn't come. With enemy soldiers almost upon me, the Misty FAC (forward air controller) coordinating rescue efforts from overhead, wisely decided that it was too dangerous to strafe.

In a life-and-death crisis, some people talk about seeing their entire life flash before them, but that was not my case. The scene that kept breaking into my consciousness during the parachute descent, and then when I was on the ground, was from the Korean War movie *The Bridges at Toko Ri*. In the movie, William Holden and Mickey Rooney play two Naval Aviators who get shot down behind enemy lines and take up a defensive position in a ditch. Surrounded by North Korean communists, they are eventually killed in a shoot-out.[4] Now I was in a similar situation, hunkering down in a bomb crater as enemy soldiers closed in. Would I suffer a similar fate? How weird it was that in the midst of the chaos of a real war, scenes from a war movie kept flitting in and out of my mind. I was determined to write a different script for my story.

In less than sixty seconds, the militia troops formed a semi-circle about thirty yards away and began moving toward me. Survival instructors had taught us that the best chance to escape is immediately after capture, because frontline soldiers are typically the least trained in handling prisoners. Deciding to try a bluff, I drew my .38-caliber, six-shot revolver (Smith and Wesson Combat Masterpiece), which was loaded with two rounds of tracer and three of regular ball ammo. Could these "rookies" be scared off? I would challenge them and find out.

The first three stepped out from the chest-high bushes and pointed their rifles at me. I raised my revolver, motioned for them to get back, and then fired a tracer round over their heads. Without flinching, they shouldered their rifles and pointed them at me. Why they didn't cut me down right then, I'll never know. I can only assume God had other plans for my life.

One of the militiamen pulled out a pamphlet. I recognized it as a "pointee talkee," a tool the Vietnamese military had devised that showed drawings of American pilots being captured, along with Vietnamese phonetics for English commands. Referring to his booklet, he began to shout, "Handsjup! Handsjup! Shurrenda no die! Shurrenda no die!"

Aviators have a number of expressions for being in deep trouble. One of the nicer ones is "out of airspeed and ideas." That precisely described my situation. To avoid the fate of the pilots in the movie at Toko Ri, my only option was to surrender. I tossed aside my pistol and raised my hands, not knowing what to expect. Immediately my captors grabbed me and began tugging at my survival vest, anti-G-suit, and flight suit—my last vestiges of protection.

Removing this specialized equipment was a learned skill, and these young militiamen, who were not familiar with zippers, resembled a pack of dogs attempting to skin a raccoon. This scene surely would have been a winner on *America's Funniest Videos*, but at the time there was nothing funny about it. I was experiencing a pilot's worst nightmare: shot down and captured in the territory of the enemy you've been bombing.

The zipper struggle was short-lived; they gave up and cut the outer layers away. Then one of them figured out how to work the main zipper, and they removed the flight suit without more damage. They next took my boots, leaving me stripped of everything except my olive drab jockey shorts. Now I really felt naked and exposed—physically, mentally, and emotionally.

Up until the time of surrender, I had operated like a computer: calculating and processing at nanosecond speed. My training "programs" had translated into almost flawless execution, a credit to the "military way" and those who did the training. Now, out of control and with no power, this cool, somewhat cocky fighter pilot felt all alone and very scared.

Captured and in enemy hands—what lay in store? Would I be tortured? Killed? The shock of my predicament made the whole affair seem like a dream. I knew this was happening to me, but I also felt like an observer, as if participating in an out-of-body experience. Unfortunately, this nightmare was real, and I would need to adopt a new mindset—a new game face—to fight a different kind of battle, a battle of minds and wills.

IT IS WITH DEEP PERSONAL CONCERN THAT I OFFICIALLY INFORM YOU THAT YOUR SON, 1ST LIEUTENANT LEON F. ELLIS, JR., IS REPORTED MISSING IN NORTH VIETNAM ON 7 NOVEMBER 1967. HE WAS A PILOT ON AN F-4C AIRCRAFT ON AN OPERATIONAL MISSION. HIS AIRCRAFT WAS LAST SEEN TO ROLL IN ON TARGET. SHORTLY THEREAFTER A LARGE FIREBALL WAS SEEN WHERE HIS AIRCRAFT PREVIOUSLY WAS LOCATED. THE FIREBALL DESCENDED TO THE GROUND AND IMPACTED. THE CREW WAS NOT SEEN TO BAIL OUT BUT, HOWEVER, VOICE CONTACT WAS ESTABLISHED WITH YOUR SON ON GROUND. RESCUE OPERATIONS ARE IN PROGRESS. LIEUTENANT ELLIS MAY HAVE BEEN CAPTURED. FOR HIS WELFARE IT IS RECOMMENDED THAT IN REPLY TO QUESTIONS OTHER THAN YOUR IMMEDIATE FAMILY YOU GIVE ONLY HIS NAME, GRADE, SERIAL NUMBER AND DATE OF BIRTH. THIS IS THE INFORMATION HE MUST PROVIDE IF CAPTURED. PLEASE BE ASSURED WHEN NEW INFORMA-TION IS RECEIVED IT WILL BE FURNISHED YOU IMMEDIATELY. A REPRESENTATIVE FROM DOBBINS AIR FORCE BASE WILL CONTACT YOU WITHIN 48 HOURS TO ASSIST IN ANY WAY POSSIBLE. IF YOU HAVE QUESTIONS YOU MAY CALL MY PERSONAL REPRESENTATIVE AT AREA CODE 512-652-3505. PLEASE ACCEPT MY SINCERE SYMPATHY DURING THIS PERIOD OF ANXIETY.

BRIGADIER GENERAL GEORGE E. MCCORD
MILITARY PERSONNEL CENTER
HEADQUARTERS UNITED STATES AIR FORCE

Telegram delivered by the USAF casualty notification officer

⑦ LESSON: KNOW YOURSELF

Near-death experiences are no fun, but they do at least cause you to stop and examine your life's priorities. Not immediately, of course; in the midst of the crisis, your only priority is survival. But later, after things calm down and the adrenaline rush subsides, you think about your family and how grateful you are to be alive. Regrets also pop into your mind—perhaps even a bit of guilt or shame—about things in your past you wish you had or hadn't done. And a lot of stuff that a few hours ago seemed so important gets pushed to the background.

In the day-to-day busyness of life, we tend to forget that we're merely passing through this world, temporary passengers on a planet we call Earth as it hurtles through this vast space we call the Universe. We expend a lot of effort trying to take control of our daily lives, and we should. An out-of-control life is of no value to anyone. But when control is suddenly lost, our minds are freed to focus on the bigger picture, and our priorities tend to get reshuffled.

Clarify Your Priorities

Fortunately, you don't need to wait until you've lost control or experienced a life-threatening crisis before you start reexamining your priorities. You can pause right now and assess whether you're living in alignment with your passion, purpose, and personality.

At the time of my capture, I was just a typical single 24-year-old exuberant pilot who had largely ignored such weighty issues. Partly because of my solid spiritual upbringing, however, I believed deeply that my life was guided toward a divine purpose. I also was passionate about my work. Since the age of five, I had felt destined to fly and to be some type of warrior. My choice of a military career as a fighter pilot was also well aligned with several of my innate personality strengths: *bold, take charge, adventurous, and challenge-driven.*

After my capture, I definitely had doubts and fears about what the next hours and days might bring, but there were no second thoughts. I had known the risks, I had made my choices, and I was committed to my cause. In short, I was authentically living "on purpose." That clarity helped me to stand firm to my values of duty, honor, and country in the days, months, and years ahead.

Connect with Your Purpose and Passion

A sense of purpose fueled by passion is essential for true success. It's fine to set your sights on any number of worthwhile goals, such as attaining a certain position of influence or making enough money for a comfortable retirement. But all of these achievements will be hollow if they don't align with an overall purpose that holds up under life-and-death scrutiny.

Clarity of purpose sharpens focus, lifts confidence, and promotes fulfillment. Unfortunately, many people are not living on purpose. Either they don't know how to uncover their purpose, or they lack the motivation to search for it. No wonder they lack energy and zest!

Hugh Massie, one of my strategic business partners, didn't stop searching until he discovered his purpose. Hugh was working for a world-renowned consulting company as a successful CPA in Singapore and Thailand when he felt drawn to educate people on finances. He moved back home to Sydney, Australia, and started his own financial services business. It was successful, but within a few years he realized that he had a more specific calling: to teach people how their natural personality responses, such as fear and risk-taking, influence their financial decisions.

That quest led Hugh to the United States, where he became a partner in the work my company was doing in the field of human behavior. Shortly thereafter, he moved to Atlanta and launched Financial DNA Resources, which is now recognized as a pioneer in the field of behavioral finance. Although Hugh is intelligent and diligent, his success in great part is due to his relentless focus on gaining clarity about his purpose.

Success is not necessarily related to money. I've worked with two executives who left successful business careers to assume key management positions with not-for-profit organizations. Both of these leaders made courageous moves in mid-life to realign their careers with their big-picture priorities.

Another of my coaching clients transitioned in mid-life in the opposite direction. "My passion is to grow business revenues and people," he told me, "and I'm stagnating here in this not-for-profit organization." Soon thereafter, he benefited himself and others by moving to a career in business that was more aligned with his temperament and desires at that stage of life.

Capitalize on Your Personality Strengths

When I first began conducting leadership training in corporations, a young man came to me at the break and asked somewhat sheepishly, "What are the best personality traits for leadership?" Intuitively, I suspected what he really wanted to know was, "Do I have the right traits to be a leader?" That question comes up in some fashion almost everywhere I go, regardless of the age of the group or the size of the organization. Recently it emerged in a training session with executives and senior leaders of a Fortune 500 company.

To illustrate different styles of leadership, I had asked this large audience to physically group themselves in the four corners of the room according to their strongest personality trait. When one participant tried to join the "highly dominant" group, he was good naturedly rejected by the other members. Somewhat disappointed, this man then joined a different group that better matched his key trait. In our debriefing after the exercise, he commented, "It's true that I don't fit with that 'dominant' group, but I've always wanted to be like them."

"Your honesty and vulnerability are admirable," I told him, "and it's not wrong for you to adapt your behaviors from time to time to be more effective in specific situations. But it is a mistake to deny your natural strengths and try to reinvent yourself to be like others. Great leaders come in a wide variety of styles and traits. The best traits for you are your innate traits, the ones you already have. You will be the best leader when you are authentic. So, be yourself.[5] The more you try to imitate others and 'pose' as someone you are not, the more difficulties you will have." This man was well respected, and the people in the room knew each other well enough to establish this kind of trust. After that experience, I'm confident he became a more authentic and effective leader.

Critical moments can be catalysts for constructive change, but I urge you not to wait for a life-and-death situation or another type of crisis before you begin to think about who you are and where you're going. Take the time now to ensure that your personal and career choices are aligned with your purpose, passion, and personality.

Living authentically enables you to wholeheartedly pursue your goals. Your energy will be greater because your focus is clearer, and your commitment will be deeper because your ownership is stronger. Instead of "doing so you can be," focus on "being so you can do." The more comfortable you are being yourself, the more productive and successful you will be.[6]

Foot Stomper: Authentic leadership flows from the inside out. You will be most successful and fulfilled when you clarify who you uniquely are in terms of purpose, passion, and personality, and then lead authentically from that core.

⑦ Coaching: KNOW YOURSELF

One of the goals for the coaching in this book is to help you become more aware of your true self. Begin that process using these questions.

1. **Consider Your Purpose.** As best you can discern, what on earth were you created to do? What are your primary goals in life? Capture in one sentence what you would like your legacy to be.

2. **Connect with Your Passion.** What activities are so satisfying that you look forward to doing them? When do you feel as if you're in "the zone"? What types of environments make you feel perfectly at home?

3. **Clarify Your Unique Personality Talents.** What are your innate personality strengths? What are your natural struggles? How will these strengths and struggles impact your career and leadership choices?[7]

Note: To download an expanded version of these coaching questions for writing your responses, visit LeadingWithHonor.com/Book.

---

[1] To view pictures of an F-4 and the one I was flying when shot down, see *Leading With Honor*, LeadingWithHonor.com/gallery.

[2] G-forces describe the impact of the centrifugal force of gravity. Normally we live in a one-G world. Positive Gs pull us toward the earth; negative Gs push us away from the earth. At five Gs a two hundred pound person weighs one thousand pounds. At some point, when the heart is unable to overcome the weight of the blood and pump it to the brain, a person will black out. Aviators are trained to fly and fight for short periods with as much as six to eight Gs. Too many negative Gs cause a red-out from blood pooling in the head and eyes. The negative Gs we experienced were enough to lift up our bodies, so that we could not achieve the proper sitting position for ejection.

[3] This original ballistic (one-shot) seat was a lifesaver, but the instantaneous explosion gave many of us back problems. Later Martin-Baker ejection seats employed a rocket seat that spread the acceleration over a longer burn time, reducing the "G" onset and its resulting compression to the spinal column.

[4] *The Bridges at Toko Ri* was based on a true story. When James Michener wrote the book in 1953, it was believed that the pilots had been killed, so that's the way he wrote it. Later it was learned that Michener's characters were captured and had survived the POW camp. I did not learn about the real storyline until recently, while doing research for this book. That also was a cause for reflection.

[5] U.S. presidents have exhibited a variety of traits. CEOs, athletic coaches, and leaders in all fields also exhibit different leadership styles, depending on their unique, innate traits.

[6] New behaviors can be learned. Effective leaders adapt their behaviors to match the situation, but they still operate primarily out of their own unique style and values.

[7] For help in learning more about your unique talents and leadership style with the *Leadership Behavior DNA™* Assessment, get started by taking the free *Leading with Honor Discovery Report* offered on page 234.

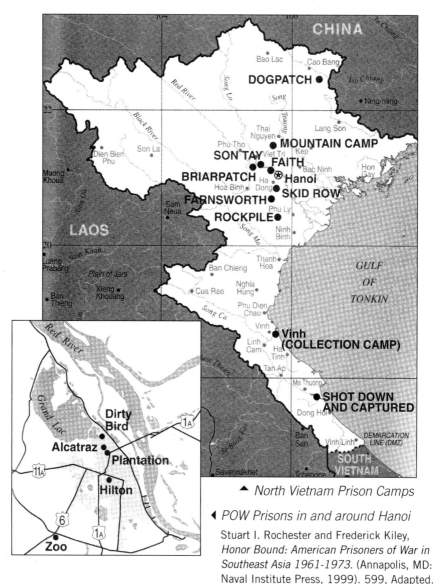

▲ *North Vietnam Prison Camps*

◀ *POW Prisons in and around Hanoi*

Stuart I. Rochester and Frederick Kiley, *Honor Bound: American Prisoners of War in Southeast Asia 1961-1973.* (Annapolis, MD: Naval Institute Press, 1999). 599, Adapted.

Chapter 2

GUARD YOUR CHARACTER

★

*"There is an ongoing battle between conscience
and self-interest in which, at some point,
we have to take sides."*

Robert Brault

A few hours after I was captured, the militia allowed me to get back into my flight suit. Then they led me—blindfolded, hands tied, and barefoot—to a nearby hamlet and shoved me down into a cave that I surmised was a bomb shelter. I thought I was alone, until I heard someone breathing heavily. "Ken, is that you?" Ken answered in the affirmative. We had time to exchange only a few sentences before they pulled me out and led me away like a dog on a leash.

On several occasions I managed to push up my blindfold, but I could see only a few feet ahead. After we had walked for an hour or so, passing by what I sensed were several small hamlets, the guards began to talk excitedly, as if something big was about to happen. Looking a few yards ahead beneath the blindfold, I observed an irrigation ditch bordering a rice paddy. With mounting fear, my emotional memory pulled up stories of the Korean War, when POWs were marched to exactly such ditches and shot. Was this the termination of my death march?

I decided I must not let them shoot me in the back. I had always had a phobia about being hit from behind. And if I faced my captors, I figured, they might lose their courage or decide to show mercy. Stopping at the ditch, I wheeled around toward the firing squad. The guards reacted with angry shouts. Through the bottom of my blindfold I saw them raise their rifles to the firing position. One guard spun me back around and cut loose with what sounded like every curse word in his repertoire.

Powered by the adrenalin that comes in a life and death struggle,

I again wheeled to face their rifles. This time they went berserk. The two guards closest to me started pummeling me and spun me around again. One of them kicked me in the butt as hard as he could, knocking me off balance. I had a choice between stumbling into the ditch or jumping over it. Instinctively, as I had done so often at the creek back home, I made a "flat-footed leap."

My safe landing on the other side miraculously broke the tension. The guards, giggling like school children, jumped over to join me. In one powerful second, fear gave way to hope. That experience provided the first installment on a lesson that would continue in the days and years ahead. My fears had been largely a product of my imagination. What I assumed was about to happen was actually very different from what they wanted to happen. I don't think I've ever been so glad to be wrong.

The journey from the southern panhandle of North Vietnam to Hanoi was a long, grueling ordeal. For the first few days they moved me from hamlet to hamlet during daylight; at night they tied me down to boards in bomb shelters. As I contemplated what suffering might lie ahead, I found encouragement in the words of the Apostle Paul: "...we also rejoice in our sufferings, because we know that suffering produces perseverance; perseverance, character; and character, hope."[1]

On three occasions American fighter jets flew in low and attacked trucks parked in the trees alongside the road. We took shelter in foxholes and bomb shelters and watched the fireworks—a front-row seat to the terrors of war. Foot-long chunks of red-hot shrapnel sometimes landed not more than six feet from me. The sights, sounds, and smells of the bombs and antiaircraft artillery explosions are indelibly etched in my memory. War attacks the emotions in a way that's impossible to describe and difficult to erase.

More threatening than the bombs were attacks from angry peasants. A mob of old women and teens, furious over the destruction American pilots had wrought, rushed toward me wielding rocks, sticks, and rice-cutting sickles. My young North Vietnamese escort and the guards under his authority formed a cordon and ushered me to safety, even absorbing some of the blows. Several times during the weeklong journey north, this young soldier saved my life. In following his orders to transport me safely, he displayed a remarkable balance of toughness and kindness, not only to me, but also to his men and to the civilians we met along the way. Strong character is remarkably apparent, even in your enemy.

My escort deposited me at the collection prison near Vinh, which was nothing more than a bamboo-pole barn divided into individual cages, each with a pile of straw on the floor for sleeping. Ken had already arrived. LtCol Ted Minter[2] and 1stLt Jim Warner, whose Marine F-4 Phantom jet had been shot down a few weeks earlier, were also there. We were kept isolated from each other and fed a small bowl of rice topped by a few greens twice a day.

A day or so after my arrival, the camp commander, whom I derogatorily nicknamed "Madman," summoned me for my first interrogation. According to the Geneva Convention, captured soldiers are required to provide name, rank, service number, and date of birth. Our Code of Conduct says that we should resist answering other questions. When I tried to stick with these "big four," Madman went berserk. He called me a criminal and threatened to kill me on the spot.

After I still refused to answer, he shouted a command in Vietnamese. A nearby guard jammed his AK-47 barrel against my head and chambered a round. Still in shock of capture and unsure of how POWs had actually been treated (all I knew was that some had been shot in Korea), I decided to talk a bit more. Spying my F-4 aircrew checklist on the table, I admitted that I had been flying the F-4 Phantom out of Danang.

Madman asked several more questions about my unit and command structure. I stalled, then gave bogus answers to a couple and "did not knows" to the rest. That was sufficient to end the interrogation without giving up any meaningful or accurate information other than the big four.

The next evening, under cover of darkness, the V (that will be my shorthand in this book for our Vietnamese captors) shoved the four of us into the back of a truck. Accompanied by several armed guards, we headed for Hanoi on bomb-crater-pocked Route 1A, the primary coastal route from north to south. With blindfolds on and hands and feet tied, we crashed up and down on the hard steel truck bed like helpless pigs going to market. Words cannot adequately describe the agony of that journey, which was heightened by the mental anguish of knowing that every bounce brought us closer to an uncertain fate in the infamous prisons of Hanoi.

At dawn our captors parked the truck in a wooded area, out of sight of the American hunter-killer pilots—our fly-buddies—who were patrolling the roads. At one point I discovered some large sacks of oranges and peanuts in the back of the truck. Although we were bound, I was able to retrieve some goodies for the four of us while the guards slept. It was a modest introduction to the tactics of survival warfare that we would use to resist and survive in the days ahead.

After another arduous night of travel, we were deposited at the Hoa Loa Prison, better known to American POWs as the "Hanoi Hilton." For several hours I sat on the nasty brick floor in a washroom and pondered what would happen next. In the late afternoon the turnkey entered, removed my blindfold and cuffs, and gave me a bowl of rice and a plate containing a large fish head.

For some reason unknown to us, this seemed to be the V's traditional meal for new prisoners. Ironically, it was a custom among some American pilots to say to each other prior to takeoff, "Be careful, or you'll be eating fish heads and rice." Although the fish head staring up at me looked rather unappetizing, a small sunken pocket behind each eye contained some of the most succulent white meat I'd ever eaten. Unfortunately, I was never fed another fish head like that during my captivity.

Just after sunset, the turnkey returned and motioned me toward the washbasin. The first bath since my capture two weeks prior was immensely uplifting, despite the shivers imparted by the ice-cold water and the chilly November air. Next I was given maroon striped boxers with matching T-shirt and the infamous "black pajamas" with my prisoner number on the shirt top. Putting on that new uniform hammered home the stark reality that I was a captured flyer incarcerated in a communist system. I never saw my flight suit again.

The turnkey, accompanied by two guards with AK-47s, ushered me to an interrogation room nearby. Ken and the two marines who had ridden up with us were already there, seated on short stools in front of a table. I was told to take the vacant stool next to them, which, like the others was intentionally short so we would have to look up to our captors. On the other side of the table sat an immaculately dressed officer, flanked by two sergeants. Pompously crossing his arms and throwing back his head with a sinister smirk, the officer said in broken English, "Now, the fat is in the fire—huh."

This unexpected declaration was so melodramatic that for a moment I felt as if I was participating in a grade-B movie. It was all I could do to keep from laughing out loud, in spite of the seriousness of the situation. Thereafter, we referred to this camp officer as "Fat in the Fire." Because his perfectly fitting uniforms always looked as if they had been tailored, we later learned that some POWs called him "The Tailor"; others called him "Little Caesar" because of his arrogance.

That evening, Fat in the Fire went on to lecture us about the "dastardly" President Johnson and the "corrupt" U.S. government. He then contrasted our "villainy" with the "lenient and humane treatment policy" of the Democratic Republic of Vietnam (DRV). As "war criminals" we were commanded to obey all orders and follow all camp rules and policies. If we did not, we would be severely punished. In the minds of our captors, disobedience justified torture.

After this indoctrination, we were escorted to a small cell that would be our home for the next several months. Hoa Loa Prison was a sprawling complex consisting of numerous buildings used as separate compounds.

Our section of the Hanoi Hilton (upper left corner of the Hanoi Hilton/Hoa Loa complex shown on page 20) was known to POWs as Little Vegas, because most Air Force fighter pilots had done some training at Nellis Air Force Base just outside Las Vegas, Nevada. The various wings of Little Vegas were appropriately named after some of the popular casino hotels of that era: Desert Inn, Stardust, Golden Nugget, Riviera, the Mint, and Thunderbird, our cellblock. Four-man cells were typical except for the Mint, which had three-and-a-half-foot by seven-foot rooms used for solitary confinement.

This is a post-war photo of Hoa Loa Prison, which American POWs called the Hanoi Hilton. It was later turned into a tourist attraction with a propaganda museum and a real hotel. The facility was not nearly so "attractive" when we were living there.

Our cell in Thunderbird was six-and-a-half feet wide and seven feet deep—about the size of a small walk-in closet—and had masonry walls sixteen inches thick. One wall faced the central courtyard of Little Vegas, and its opposite wall fronted the main hallway. The side walls of our cell were separated from the walls of the neighboring cells by narrow hallways, so we could not tap messages through them to other POWs. Camp rules (see Appendix C) tacked to the inside of our cell made it clear that anyone communicating with another cell would be severely punished. Armed guards constantly patrolled the halls to ensure compliance.

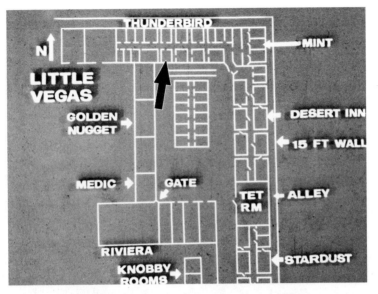

The Little Vegas section of the Hanoi Hilton
The arrow points to my cell in Thunderbird.

The heavy door of our cell had an 8" X 10" peephole with a hinged cover, which guards occasionally would flip open to threaten us and make sure we were behaving ourselves. There were four "beds" about thirty inches wide, made from 2" X 6" boards that were bracketed two-high to the walls on either side of the doorway. The walking space between the bunk beds measured about eighteen inches. From the high ceiling hung a single dim light bulb that burned night and day. Iron leg stocks at the foot of the beds gave this dark and depressing cell the ominous feel of a medieval dungeon.

At least three times a day, seven days a week, the V piped in propaganda through a box speaker (also called the "camp radio") attached high on one wall. When the commentators boasted about how President Ho Chi Minh had set the Vietnamese people free, they naturally didn't mention that "Uncle Ho" had used his absolute power to eliminate most freedoms and forcibly "reeducate" or entirely eradicate the farmers and landowners who had resisted confiscation of their property.

Just before bedtime Hanoi Hannah, the North Vietnamese version of the infamous Tokyo Rose of World War II, shared communist half-truths and outright lies. She typically closed her broadcast each night in a sympathetic and sisterly tone by saying, "GIs, why should you die ten thousand miles from home? Lay down your arms now and cross over to the people's side."

The afternoon broadcasts were especially disheartening because they featured Americans spouting words that could have been written for them in Hanoi or Moscow. Tom Hayden, founder of the socialist front organization, Students for a Democratic Society (SDS), was a regular speaker. Later in the war, the V welcomed the aid of Hayden's antiwar-activist wife, film star Jane Fonda.

Isolated in that tiny cell, the four of us had plenty of time to get to know each other.[3] Capt Fisher told us how he had endured brutal torture during his initial interrogation back at Vinh to avoid answering any questions beyond the big four. At Madman's command, guards had tied his arms behind his back, tossed a rope over a high beam, and pulled Ken's arms up and behind, lifting him until he was suspended with the weight of his body pulling and tearing at the muscles, ligaments, and nerves in his shoulders.

A star collegiate wrestler and New York state high school champion, Ken was mentally and physically one of the toughest men I'd ever known. But eventually the pain transformed him into "a screaming idiot." As we all learned to do, he had to fall back to a second line of resistance. At times some POWs prayed for death as a relief, but the V, who were experts at torture, rarely obliged.

Upon hearing Ken's story, I felt embarrassed and immature. He had suffered so much trying to follow the strict letter of the Code, while I had given in after threats and a rifle jab to the head. When I shared my interrogation encounter with him, he said with sincere kindness, "You did the best you could under the circumstances. We ended up at the same place, giving them something that was nothing." That experience gave me a glimpse of the character of this man who would be a cellmate and inspirational leader for the next five years.

LtCol Minter was summoned to more interrogations than the rest of us. That seemed natural at first; as the senior ranking officer (SRO) in our room, he was potentially the highest value target for exploitation. But over time we realized that Minter's views were not aligned with ours or with the policy of our government. A soldier has an obligation to do his best to uphold the Code of Conduct, which includes resisting exploitation by the enemy. What might be acceptable for a civilian back home in our free society is totally out of line for a military person, especially a POW.

One day Minter came back from an interrogation with pencil and paper and began writing an extensive description of the organization and responsibilities of a Marine air wing. We cautioned him that his cooperation was a violation of the Code of Conduct, but he said he didn't see any problem. Later when he was called out of the room for an interrogation, we looked at the paper and saw that it contained information that appeared accurate and of value to the enemy, a clear breach of the Code. Capt Fisher, as the next senior officer in the cell, told Lieutenant Warner and me that he felt compelled to remove LtCol Minter from command. He asked if we agreed.

It is a very serious and risky step for a captain to relieve a lieutenant colonel of command. If competent authority did not support Ken's action, he would likely face a court-martial for insubordination. We also risked court-martial for our involvement. But we knew Ken was right, so we gave him our wholehearted support.

When Minter returned to the room, Ken said, "Your willing cooperation with the enemy in writing this paper is a violation of the Code of Conduct. I am removing you from command and ordering you to destroy that document and cease cooperating with the enemy. If you disobey these orders, I will personally seek a court-martial against you after the war."

Minter said he did not believe the Code of Conduct applied in this case, because we were not in a declared war. In his opinion, everyone was free to do as he saw fit. That was a shockingly irresponsible attitude for a military officer. Only a few months previous, he had told friends

Military Code of Conduct

I

I am an American, fighting in the forces which guard my country and our way of life. I am prepared to give my life in their defense.

II

I will never surrender of my own free will. If in command, I will never surrender the members of my command while they still have the means to resist.

III

If I am captured, I will continue to resist by all means available. I will make every effort to escape and aid others to escape. I will accept neither parole nor special favors from the enemy.

IV

If I become a prisoner of war, I will keep faith with my fellow prisoners. I will give no information or take part in any action which might be harmful to my comrades. If I am senior, I will take command. If not, I will obey the lawful orders of those appointed over me, and will back them up in every way.

V

When questioned, should I become a prisoner of war, I am required to give only name, rank, service number, and date of birth. I will evade answering further questions to the utmost of my ability. I will make no oral or written statements disloyal to my country and its allies or harmful to their cause.[4]

VI

I will never forget that I am an American, fighting for freedom, responsible for my actions, and dedicated to the principles which made my country free. I will trust in my God and in the United States of America.

he "hoped to make general." Now his comments made him look like a selfish survivor who would forsake his beloved Corps, his friends, his roommates, and even his country to save his hide.

That evening LtCol Minter ripped up the document and threw it in the waste bucket. But his behaviors over subsequent years indicated that he never had a change of heart. Thankfully, we were moved away to the Son Tay camp, about twenty miles northwest of Hanoi, a few months later, and we never saw him again. (see map in Appendix A) We did hear his voice on the camp radio, however, when he and his cellmate shared a disgusting pro-Hanoi, anti-war perspective. After moving back to the Hanoi Hilton in 1970, we learned that Minter had refused to cooperate with and even ratted on fellow POWs who were trying to communicate in his cellblock.[5]

To my knowledge, this was the only time during our captivity that a junior officer took command from a more senior one. It was a risky decision that required wisdom and strength of character. Later, when senior officers in the camp learned of these circumstances, they totally supported Ken's actions and commended him for his courage.

How differently these two men viewed their commitments! LtCol Minter stood by his obligations as long as doing so served his personal interests. But when it required personal sacrifice and suffering, he scuttled everything else to protect himself. Minter had some good qualities, but he was not authentic and he did not lead with honor. When put to the test, fear won out over character, and rationalization trumped fidelity.

On the other hand, Capt Ken Fisher stood faithful, risking his career by stripping the colonel of command. Later, as our cell SRO, he endured torture and humiliation to resist enemy exploitation. Fisher's principled bravery was a powerful example for the rest of us.

⑦ LESSON: GUARD YOUR CHARACTER

What causes one person to abandon his commitments even before he's seriously tested, and another to keep his commitments nearly to the point of death? I'm quite certain both Fisher and Minter would say they were men of high integrity, but obviously they had vastly different views of what integrity means. One had real clarity about his values and a very strong commitment to keep them. The other was committed to his values as long as keeping them was convenient. When the going got tough, he found it easy to rationalize his way around his values by saying that war had never been declared.

Stay Connected to Truth

Often people ask me why the V so readily resorted to torture. My answer is that the communist system is founded on the belief that the end justifies the means. When they tortured half the guys in my camp to try to force them to sign public statements saying they had received "humane treatment," they saw no disconnect, because their concept of truth was derived from their ideology, not the other way around. Their allegiance was to the party line, not to real truth. In fact, one of the interrogators told us that "truth is that which most benefits the party." A system based on such a significant flaw regarding integrity and honor can only survive on power and fear, reinforced by constant misinformation.

Unfortunately, this same "end-justifies-the-means" mentality is becoming increasingly prevalent in our American culture. Business leaders are far too willing to cut corners to advance their organizations' goals and their own careers. Greed is rampant on Wall Street. Politicians regularly make statements they know aren't totally true and issue promises they don't intend to keep. Confidence in the accuracy of media reporting is at an all-time low. To make matters worse, the rest of the citizenry are more and more inclined to excuse such behaviors as "the way things are done these days." We should expect our leaders and institutions to tell the truth, keep commitments, and consistently walk their talk. We must hold leaders accountable to lead with honor, and we should start with ourselves.

Stay on Course with Your Commitments and Values

While pursuing a master's degree in counseling and human development, I had an opportunity to conduct intake interviews at the federal prison at Maxwell Air Force Base in Montgomery, Alabama. At that time, this prison without walls was populated chiefly by white-collar criminals. Just prior to my arrival, the inmates included former Attorney General John Mitchell of Watergate fame. During my tenure, the former governor of Kentucky, along with numerous other politicians, preachers, bankers, stockbrokers—and even a judge from my hometown—were there.

It was both insightful and scary to see how easily these men had veered off course. For most, it was a gradual process. Little by little their behaviors departed from their values. Unfortunately, they didn't periodically check their compass, and they didn't have people holding them accountable.

Dr. Gordon MacDonald, a prominent, well-respected pastor and Christian leader, fell into this trap. The author of several popular books, including one on marriage, he told a friend that he was sure he would never commit marital infidelity. Yet within a few years of making that statement, he confessed to an extramarital affair.

"A chain of seemingly innocent choices became destructive," he said later, "and it was my fault. Choice by choice by choice: each easier to make, each becoming gradually darker. And then my world broke—in the very area I had predicted I was safe...." MacDonald has since repented, reconciled with his wife, and been restored to ministry. Although this one incident clouded his life and career, his openness about it has provided a good lesson for us all.

I can still remember the day when I heard MacDonald's story on the radio. I was driving north out of Atlanta on I-85 and it shook me to the core. If it could happen to him, it could happen to anyone, even me. The message came through loud and clear that our best protection comes from being humbly aware of our vulnerability, and then guarding our character with an unwavering commitment. As MacDonald later observed, "If you have been burned as deeply as I (and my loved ones) have, you never live a day without remembering that there is something within that, if left *unguarded* (italics mine), will go on the rampage."

To drive home the point about our vulnerability in the area of character, let's look at a more recent failure by a high-profile leader. Football coach Jim Tressel is famous for his sterling record and for winning a national championship at Ohio State. Widely regarded for his image as a gentleman, he has even written books on character and faith. So it was especially shocking when he admitted that he had intentionally misled NCAA investigators, and that he violated his employment contract by not reporting violations by his players. In a press conference Tressel explained that he did not disclose his failings because he was afraid of what might happen to his players. Further, he indicated that he did not know who to talk to about the situation. Tressel's story vividly reminds us that even those with the strongest character are at risk when they are operating alone and controlled by fear.

Stay Close to a Few Whom You Trust

Reliably keeping commitments and consistently living espoused values is always challenging. Our moral compass can easily drift away from true north, and our actions can veer off course almost before we realize it. We need a support team, a few trusted friends with whom we can be totally vulnerable and transparent.

Bill George, former CEO of Medtronic and author of the best selling book *True North: Discover Your Authentic Leadership*, strongly believes that authentic leaders who want to remain authentic need the support of a team. George learned nearly thirty years ago the important role a small support group can play and personally has stayed connected. In interviews with a broad cross-section of authentic leaders, he found that most of them had leaned heavily on a few confidants to keep them focused on their authentic "true north."

Character is foundational for trust, and trust is the most essential ingredient for leadership influence. People don't want to follow leaders they can't trust. Guard your character, protect your honor, and stay on course.

Foot Stomper: Authentic leaders intentionally guard their character. Clarify your values with specificity and total honesty. Then structure a support team to help you live your commitments with courage and transparency.

⑦ Coaching: GUARD YOUR CHARACTER

Good character is a purposeful decision. You cannot assume it will just happen. Intentionally guard and cultivate your character by taking the following steps.

1. **Clarify your values**. Human nature is naturally drawn toward selfishness, pride, and fear. Write out short statements clarifying your character values as non-negotiable commitments. Need help in clarifying your values? Download my Honor Code at www.LeadingWithHonor.com/Book.

2. **Examine your behaviors.** Are your life and your leadership endeavors in congruence with your values and beliefs? Recall a challenge to your character that you met successfully. What enabled you to stand firm with your commitments? Recall a missed opportunity, such as a broken promise or a time when you failed to live up to your commitments. What pulled you off course? What did you learn from this experience?

3. **Seek accountability.** You cannot maintain good character alone. Do you have a few trustworthy confidants with whom you can be transparent and vulnerable? If not, how could you develop those relationships?

4. **Walk your talk**. Are you intentionally modeling character at work and at home? What are you doing to pass along your values to others?

Note: To download an expanded version of these coaching questions for writing your responses, visit LeadingWithHonor.com/Book.

---

[1] Rom 5:3-4 (New International Version).

[2] Minter is a fictitious name.

[3] Outside the small cells in the Hanoi Hilton, the guards were always patrolling the halls trying to catch us communicating, so we had to talk just above a whisper. If they could hear us outside, they would bang on the door. If we continued to talk in a normal voice, they would pull us out for "punishment."

[4] After the war DOD removed the word "only" from Article 5 for clarification. Concern over the "big four" was eliminated, but the general requirement to avoid giving information remains.

[5] VADM Stockdale, senior ranking Naval POW, pursued court-martial for Minter after the war, but the senior civilian leaders in the Department of Defense overruled him. The political leaders believed that with the release of POWs it was time to heal the wounds of the war in our country. It was assumed that a trial would have given the radical anti-war groups one more opportunity to challenge the legality of the war, thus further dividing the country.

Chapter 3

STAY POSITIVE

*"Everything can be taken from a man or a woman
but one thing: the last of human freedoms –
to choose one's attitude in any given
set of circumstances...."*

Victor Frankl

Life for the POW was primitive. Our "possessions" consisted of a one-liter clay water pitcher, a blanket, a mosquito net, two sets of black pajamas and underwear, a toothbrush, a tube of Vietnamese toothpaste to last three months, a tin cup, a bar of lye soap, a small hand towel, and some squares of heavy brown paper to use as toilet tissue. Our "bathroom" was a three-gallon bucket in the corner of the cell.

The wake-up gong rang daily at 6:00 a.m. Our primary turnkey, whom we had nicknamed "Sweet Pea," escorted one of us down the hall to the sewer opening for the daily bucket dump. To him this duty was offensive, but to us it was a welcomed opportunity to check out the surroundings and try to contact our neighbors when the guards looked the other way.

A few weeks after our arrival, an officer escorted a medic into our cell. He had the demeanor of an absent-minded professor and wore a steel helmet, as if expecting an air raid, so we nicknamed him "Combat Medic." After inspecting the room, Combat Medic pointed to our bare bed boards and said to the officer, "No mattress?" We all suffered from sore hips from sleeping on the hard lumber, so our spirits soared when the officer promised to correct the deficiency. But our elation was short-lived, because the mattresses that arrived the next day were nothing more than rice-straw mats about an eighth of an inch thick. Even today, many of the former POWs have arthritis in their hip joints, and some have had hip replacements.

Normally, the V let us out of our tiny cell only fifteen minutes a day, five or six days a week, but never on Sunday because that was their day off. We were allowed to spend ten minutes in the washhouse bathing and washing clothes, and about two and a half minutes retrieving each of our two daily meals from the hallway outside our cell. About once a week we were allowed to shave—or rather "torment"—our faces with a 1960's-era blade that had been used previously by ten or twenty other scruffy POWs. Except for a one-hour siesta after lunch, we were not allowed to lie down or sleep during the day. Some of the men became adept at sleeping while seated, leaning against a wall.

For the first two years the feeling of hunger never left us. Food was the most popular topic of conversation, especially when it was cold and our bodies needed more calories just to stay warm. Upon awakening in the winter months, I would realize I had been dreaming about walking down a cafeteria line selecting a breakfast of eggs, bacon, sausage, toast, orange juice, and coffee. But in reality, our typical meal was a bowl of thin, greasy vegetable soup, accompanied by either a cup of rice or an eight-inch baguette of bread.

We joked that the menu had lots of variety; it changed three times a year. Six months of the year we dined on pumpkin soup, followed by three months of cabbage soup, followed by three months of an aquatic vegetable we called sewer greens. One summer we kept a record: for forty-four straight days, two meals a day, we ate pumpkin soup embellished with a side dish (two tablespoons) of stewed pumpkins. We called this meal "pumpkin squared."

It required a sense of humor to eat this "ghoulish" goulash. Often it contained a small chunk of pork fat, complete with the pig's skin and hair, or a small amount of dog meat that tasted somewhat like Italian sausage. Occasionally, unexpected "delicacies" would appear. For instance, a fellow in the adjoining cell found a pig's eye in his soup one day, and another POW found a monkey's hand.

Since the V cooked outside in big pots, small bugs and white worms would regularly drop into the soup from overhanging trees. Every August weevils would hatch in the flour, so the bread would be peppered with the black buggers. Having nothing better to do one afternoon, I counted forty-four in one cubic inch of bread. There were too many to pick out, so we just ate them, figuring they were a good source of protein.

I was thankful that the primary meals came as soup dishes. They were boiled, which meant they were relatively free from germs, and they contained sufficient nutrients to keep us alive. They also provided much-needed fluids to supplement our one liter of water per day. The bread with each meal provided most of the protein in our diet, and the baked-in bugs were a bonus.

When the sun went down, the rats came out in droves. You could see them scurrying back and forth along walls and up and down tree limbs, not unlike columns of ants. One night when I was sleeping on the floor, an eight-inch rat (they typically were six to eight inches in length, not including the tail) came through a drainage vent and became trapped between my mosquito net and the cell wall. As it wildly thrashed about, I felt as if I were battling a medium-sized cat. I'm not sure which of us was more scared. My personal rat experience was far from the worst in the camps, though. One POW who had been severely injured during ejection from his aircraft awoke in the middle of the night to find rats chewing on his mangled, infected leg. He fought them off, but they came back. There was always an ongoing rat skirmish of some sort.

Winters in Hanoi are surprisingly cold, with temperatures often in the low forties Fahrenheit, and sometimes lower. The chilly air blowing in through our barred open window, covered only with a rattan mat, made our unheated cell feel like an icebox. It was also cold because our meager rations provided insufficient energy to stay warm through the long nights. We survived by putting on every bit of clothing we owned—two pairs of thin pajamas and a cotton sweater—and wrapping ourselves in our blanket. For the first two years we had no socks, so our feet never got warm in winter.[1]

Fat in the Fire opened our peephole one day and asked how we were doing. We told him we were cold at night and needed more blankets and food. He snapped, "This is prison, not hotel!" Did he know that in our gallows humor we called the prison "The Hanoi Hilton"? We never found out.

The POW experience produced severe mental and emotional stress. Hour after hour we found ourselves battling an army of oppressive feelings—from fear about what might happen to us, to anger at our captors for the way they treated us, to disappointment for being shot down, to guilt for leaving our families in the lurch and in the dark. Maintaining a positive mental outlook was crucial to survival.

Military leaders expect life to be difficult, yet they tend to be optimistic about their capability to succeed. They are trained to make the best of the situation by solving problems instead of stewing about them, and they place a high value on cohesive teamwork. Fortunately, that's the kind of leadership we had in Hanoi.

A few of our buddies who had more pessimistic temperaments occasionally needed extra measures of encouragement from the rest of us. In return, they frequently contributed a healthy dose of realism that balanced our optimism with objectivity and discipline. Vice Admiral James Bond Stockdale insightfully captured the importance of this dynamic tension in what Jim Collins called the "Stockdale Paradox":

> "You must never confuse faith that you will prevail in the end—which you can never afford to lose—with the discipline to confront the most brutal facts of your current reality, whatever they might be."[2]

When you are at the mercy of an enemy who has the power to force you to do things against your will, the psychological impact can be unimaginably depressing and debilitating. His goal is to break you, and you must constantly fight to maintain your self-respect and optimism. Most of us did this in two primary ways.

First, we fought to maintain our belief in ourselves and our competency by resisting the enemy and exercising our autonomy at every opportunity. In order to demonstrate that our lives still had worth and that we were not helpless, we had to find ways to get our licks in, often using tricks and subtle acts of rebellion as weapons. Every time a POW outsmarted the V, no matter how trivial the incident, other POWs were encouraged and emboldened.

When forced to make propaganda statements, we would often use a hoax or subtleties of the English language to undermine the enemy. For example, after extensive torture, a Navy crew "confessed" that two men in their squadron were being court-martialed for refusing to fly combat missions over North Vietnam. The names of the two men, they said, were LT Clark Kent (familiar to Americans as Superman) and LCDR Ben Casey (from the Dr. Ben Casey TV show). One Air Force pilot wrote in his forced "confession" that he was "sorry for the miserable Vietnamese people." Another wrote "...that he regretted coming to Vietnam because the people had been 'truly revolting for four thousand years.'"[3] (To compare military ranks see Appendix F.)

We were not allowed to yell out or even talk loudly, but one POW would routinely hurl a disguised in-your-face insult to the V by belting out a gigantic sneeze: "horsssss-shit." It was so loud that it echoed up and down the hallways of Thunderbird, lifting our morale and giving us a much-needed laugh. Not to be outdone, another POW who had been tortured to read propaganda on the camp radio, pronounced the name of their esteemed leader "Horse-shit-minh." I still don't know who did that, but he should have been given a medal—maybe an Oscar—for that performance.

When the V tried to exploit Navy LT Paul Galanti by photographing him in a spacious, airy room specially prepared for propaganda purposes, he "flipped them the finger"—literally. As the photo was taken, Paul subtly rested both hands on the end of the bed with his middle fingers pointing down. At the time, the V did not realize that Paul had outwitted them, and some socialist country journalists unknowingly used the photo as it was. Others caught it and completely airbrushed out his fingers. Fortunately, an original copy made it back to the U.S., where Paul's intended message came through loud and clear: "This is a big propaganda lie."[4]

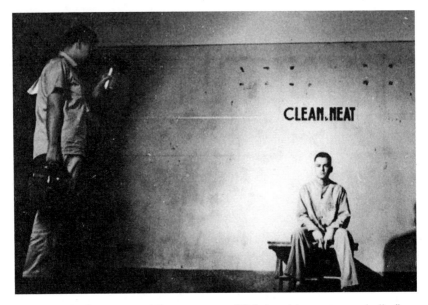

Galanti's fingers send the message: "This is a big propaganda lie."

Another way we fought to maintain our dignity was to carry on guerrilla warfare with the guards and lower-level interrogators who often stopped by our cells to harass us or practice their English. Our efforts varied from showing a disrespectful attitude through harsh words and belligerent body language, to devious tricks to make them uncomfortable.

To keep the guards who most irritated us from opening our peephole and yelling insults, we would move the toilet bucket up next to the door of our cell and remove the lid. When the belligerent guard came by and snatched open the peephole to look in, he would inhale a stench much worse than the foulest porta potty. After the guard slammed the door and skedaddled, we would burst into muffled laughter. Even the smallest victories were important in this war of wills.

At other times we would refuse to bow to guards, turnkeys, and officers. They responded with slaps, interrogations, threats of torture, and other punishments. Once when we refused to bow, the V closed all of our air vents and kept us locked in our cell without an outside bath for several weeks. The sweltering conditions—100°F heat and high humidity—gave us heat rash and boils, but it was worth it.

Faith was also a primary source of strength, dignity, and hope. We had faith in each other, in our leaders, in our country, in our families, and especially in God. The old saying that "there are no atheists in foxholes" was certainly true in the POW camps. As I mentioned earlier, I knew God loved me unconditionally, and that He had a plan for my life. Although I didn't have a Bible in the early years, the POW environment seemed to significantly sharpen my memory, and I could recall many of my favorite scripture verses. Romans 8:28—"In all things God works for the good of those who love Him, who have been called according to His purpose"—and other passages, like Psalms 1, 23, and 100, gave me an inner strength and a sense of peace that kept me going.

In his book *Before Honor*, here's how former POW CAPT Eugene (Red) McDaniel, USN, described his battle for survival and the attitude that many of us held:

> "...If there was something to be lived in this sordid atmosphere of pain, then I had to live it. To abandon hope, the possibility of survival, meant I would lose possession of myself, my own worth, my own self-identity. In that case, the North Vietnamese had won—their intent was to destroy finally that sense of worth we all needed to hang on to. .... So every day was a battle to stay alive in a hopeless situation and resist my captor's attempts to exploit my weaknesses and break me. I sensed that to give in to them was to surrender a big chunk of what God was trying to instill in me.... All I had was tomorrow, and maybe that was the height of optimism. Well then, I would make tomorrow count for something—and on that, I finally found sleep."[5]

In addition to the living conditions and threats, there was the continual stress of being in a strange environment apart from our loved ones. But gradually, as we settled into this new life, we gained confidence that we would survive. We learned to live one day at a time. The consistently positive attitude of our leaders set the tone, giving us hope that someday we would go home to our families and country.

⑦ LESSON: STAY POSITIVE

POWs are not alone in facing hardships. All leaders face difficulties and challenges every day. None of us can control what the next day will bring, but there is one thing we all can control: our attitude. Attitude is crucial for success in any endeavor, and no one influences organizational and individual attitudes more than the leader.

Leaders Face Adversity with a Positive Attitude

Although it's not easy to turn lemons into lemonade, leaders must strive to do just that by maintaining a positive attitude. We have to expect that we're going to be handed lemons, sour grapes, rotten deals, and unfair decisions. How we deal with them is the true test of our leadership. Because leaders have such a powerful influence on others, they don't have the luxury of wallowing in negativity and self-pity.

Attitude was not a problem for me as a POW. I believed that some day we would return and things would be okay. Actually, I had more difficulty with attitude after I returned home to the "real world," because I expected everything to run smoothly all the time. Of course, that was not the case, and I had to learn to adjust.

As a young flying squadron commander, I had the privilege of leading a select group of T-38 instructor pilots (IPs), all of whom had one thousand or more hours of instructor time in the aircraft. They were mostly the cream of the crop, and they helped us garner a reputation of excellence. One day in the midst of our normal flying operations, two officers from the Inspector General (IG) team arrived and set up shop in one of our offices.

It turned out that they were conducting a follow-up investigation on an accident that had occurred at another base. The instructors responsible for the accident had been trained in our squadron three years prior. They were flying an unauthorized maneuver at the time of the accident, so the investigators were looking for a thread of deviancy that might trace back to our unit, even though their training had occurred before any of my guys had arrived on station.

Because the IG was involved, as opposed to the accident board, the investigation had the feel of a hunting expedition that was looking for a scapegoat. Moreover, I felt that their approach of interrogating our instructor pilots under oath would hurt morale and interfere with our focus on flight operations. (It didn't occur to me at the time, but in retrospect I can see that my anger might have been aroused by my emotional memory of abuses in interrogations I experienced as a POW.)

When I complained to my boss, he gave me a frustrated look and said, "Lee, anyone can steer the ship through the calm waters. The real captains take it through the storms." His powerful statement hit me like a sledgehammer. It was a great lesson that inspires me to this day. Leaders take others through the difficult times, and to do that they must engage even negative and "unfair" situations with a positive attitude. On the way back to the squadron, I revamped my attitude and accepted the challenge. We sailed through that little storm with ease.

Leaders Recognize that Emotions are Contagious

Most of us have heard the jocular expression, "If the boss (or Momma) ain't happy, then nobody's happy." In my experience, that observation has proved to be true time and again. Research in the last twenty years verifies that emotions are contagious.[6] A poor attitude is like a disease, and it can spread like an epidemic. Just as a rock splashing in a pond sends out ripples over a wide area, a bad attitude can quickly contaminate an entire organization.

One of my healthcare clients had a doctor on staff whose poor attitude was so adversely affecting the morale of the nurses that I was brought in to help. It turned out that this doctor's mood set the tone for the entire staff. If he was in a good mood when he walked in the unit in the morning, the atmosphere stayed light and positive all day. But if he was in a foul mood, which was often the case, the air was thick with gloom, cynicism, and criticism. It was a shame this doctor had such a sour personality, because he had great medical skills and exhibited compassion toward his patients. But his negative attitude was creating a near-hostile environment. Eventually, after several unsuccessful attempts to remedy the situation, he was removed.

Leaders Lead Through Change

Most people fear change and tend to resist it. But in today's workplace, where change is occurring at an increasingly rapid rate, leaders must have a strategy to address the negative emotions it evokes.

Brian Shield, executive vice president and chief information officer at the Weather Channel, is an impressive leader who understands the impact of change on morale. When this privately held company was offered for sale in 2008, Brian proactively began preparing his managers so they could lead their people through a difficult time of uncertainty. Knowing they were likely to be bought by a Fortune 500 company, Brian sensed the fears that were building: potential loss of job, reorganization with a change in manager, change of office, loss of peers, and unpredictable cultural changes that were sure to come. He asked us to help prepare his leaders to lead and to coach their people through the changes that were occurring.

An important part of the "leading in change" curriculum we provided to the Weather Channel focused on emotional intelligence training for Brian's team of IT leaders. They gained a new understanding of how emotions impact the workplace, and they learned how effective leaders manage their own emotions and recognize and respond appropriately to the emotional needs of others. The company was acquired a few months later, and many changes did indeed take place. However, because of Brian's foresight, poise, and personal involvement in this preparation, the IT team remained focused and productive during a challenging period of transition.

Motivational speakers and leadership books focus more on attitude than anything else, because it is the most essential element of success.

Yes, diligence and dedication are important, but inspiration is the source of power. Commander Stockdale was right: "faith that we would prevail" is the essential "first principle" of successful leadership. It enabled us to resist and survive as POWs and return with honor. This same "possibility thinking" enables poor men to become rich, sick people to become well, last-place teams to become first, and each of us to reach our potential as human beings and leaders.

Foot Stomper: A positive attitude is one of a leader's greatest assets, and it's one of the best ways you can influence/lead others. Keep your chin up, because when it goes down, you do too, and many others will follow right behind.

⑦ Coaching: STAY POSITIVE

As a leader, you must find a positive way to deal with the negative issues that come your way. Use these insights and questions to reflect on your attitude and its impact on your influence.

1. **Engage adversity with a positive attitude.**
   How do you respond when life is not fair? How could you engage challenges more effectively? In what ways do you respond differently to your manager from how you respond to your direct reports or peers?

2. **Manage your emotions as if they're contagious, because they are.**
   What situations have you observed where your negative emotions affected others? How could you handle your negative emotions more productively? Where can you start?

3. **Engage change with a plan.**
   Do you intentionally develop plans for dealing with change?
   What books have you read on the subject of leading through change?[7]
   What other resources do you use in developing strategies for dealing with change?

Note: To download an expanded version of these coaching questions for writing your responses, visit LeadingWithHonor.com/Book.

---

[1] Many of us have nerve damage to our feet from the long periods of exposure to the cold.

[2] Jim Collins, *Good To Great*. (New York, NY: Harper Collins, 2001) 86-88.

[3] Brig Gen Jon Reynolds, interview by Lee Ellis, "POW Leadership," September 16, 2007.

[4] Unfortunately, the version of the photo on the cover of *LIFE Magazine*, Oct 20, 1967 was courtesy of a communist East German photographer, and all the fingers had been carefully airbrushed out.

[5] Eugene B. McDaniel and James L. Johnson, *Before Honor*. (Philadelphia, PA: A.J. Holman Company, 1975) 63-64.

[6] Daniel Goleman, PhD uses the research on emotional intelligence as the basis for several of his best-selling books on the subject. I often refer to his book *Primal Leadership* and recommend it to my clients.

[7] Consider books like *Leading Change* and *The Heart of Change* by John P. Kotter, and *Switch* by Chip Heath and Dan Heath.

Chapter 4

CONFRONT YOUR
DOUBTS AND FEARS

*"He who is not everyday conquering some
fear has not learned the secret of life."*

Ralph Waldo Emerson

A few months after arriving in the Hanoi Hilton, an English-speaking turnkey casually delivered copies of a three-page biographical question-naire to our cell and told each of us to fill one out. It contained detailed questions about family, socioeconomic background, education, and military experience, including assignments and training. If accurately completed, these biographies could give our captors valuable insights they could use for propaganda and psychological warfare. They would also reveal who among us might have had access to sensitive military information. When the turnkey returned to pick them up, we told him that we were providing the basic information required under Geneva Convention, but no more. He left in a huff.

We waited anxiously, knowing that they were not going to let us off the hook. The next day when we heard the keys rattling outside our door at an odd time in the daily schedule, my stomach tightened in a knot. The door opened and our regular turnkey Sweet Pea motioned for Ken and me to suit up into our long-sleeve black pajamas. Then he took us out separately to different interrogation rooms. It was again time to confront my doubts and fears.

The interrogator took the "I'm your friend" approach. After politely asking me some questions about my living conditions and health, "Good Buddy" (our nickname for him) said in a reassuring manner, "I understand you may not want to fill out the questionnaire, but as your friend I advise you to do it. It's a camp requirement. You are a 'creeminal' and must obey all orders of the camp officers."

When I again refused, Good Buddy suddenly transformed before my eyes. His voice became shrill, the veins popped out on his head and neck, and he yelled, "If you do not obey my orders, another man will come and torture you very badly!" I still refused, so he ordered me to sit on a small stool; then he left me alone in the room to think about it.

After an hour or so, Good Buddy returned and again ordered me to comply. When I refused, guards shackled my legs and forced me to get down on my knees with my arms over my head. I was warned that if I moved from that position, I would be beaten. It didn't take long before my knees and muscles were in agony and my arms felt like lead. About three hours later, Good Buddy returned and threatened me with "terrible torture, even electric shock to the heart." I was then left alone in the stress position to reconsider. In the hours that followed, I had to battle minute by minute with all my strength against two enemies: my captors and my internal doubts and fears.

POW on his knees for the "humane torture"[1]
Drawing by former POW Mike McGrath

During the long night I often had to lower my arms or sit down. When the guards caught me, they kicked me and forced me back into position. Although this type of torture was no doubt preferable to the harsher alternatives, I could see why the V used it. In addition to leaving no marks on the body, it forced us in a manner of speaking to inflict the torture on ourselves. I knew they were to blame for this inhumane treatment, but I could not escape the fear that at some point I also would be guilty too, if I was not strong enough or tough enough to endure the pain I was inflicting on myself.

Around 6:00 a.m. a new interrogator entered the room and ordered me to complete the form. When I refused, he told the guard to stay with me and beat me whenever I moved out of the stress position. Around 8:00 a.m. I dropped to the floor, too exhausted to remain in position. The guard began kicking and hitting me with increasing intensity. Finally I yelled, "Bao Cao," indicating that I wanted to speak to the officer in charge.

After I had filled in the biography questions with false and misleading information, I was left lying on the floor in irons and handcuffs for another hour or so. It was probably the lowest point in my life. My fatigued and aching body bore little semblance to the strong, brave image I formerly had of myself. Though I had not cooperated or given anything of value, I felt miserably ashamed and totally defeated, like the weakest, most worthless officer ever to wear the uniform.

A short while later a guard brought food and water into the room and removed the cuffs and leg irons. After I had eaten, I was returned to my cell. Ken showed up an hour or so later. He had gone through a similar experience and also had filled out the forms with contrived answers. We consoled each other with the knowledge that we had done our best by forcing them to use torture to gain any compliance, while denying them what they wanted. In time we learned that virtually every POW in the camp had gone through this ordeal with the same outcome. Now our job was to bounce back for another round of resistance the next time the keys came rattling at our door.[2]

Although we all endured hardships, few suffered more than Naval

Aviator Lieutenant Commander John McCain. A college wrestler and somewhat of a firebrand, he was probably the most severely wounded POW who lived to return home. During ejection and capture, his right arm was broken in three places; his left arm and right leg were broken; he sustained a football-size hematoma on one leg; and he suffered bayonet wounds and blows to the head. He probably would have died in captivity, but when the V read in the *Stars and Stripes*, the Pacific military newspaper, that he was the son of a four-star admiral, they kept him alive for potential propaganda value.

In 1968, "Cat"—that was our name for the communist political boss in charge of POWs— met with McCain and told him he would be released. The V had conducted an "early release" of three men earlier in the year as a ploy to convince the world of their "lenient and humane" treatment of POWs. Our internal guidelines stipulated that all POWs would return home in the order in which they were captured (first in, first out), except sick and wounded POWs were allowed to go first. Considering his lingering serious injuries, it was a difficult choice. McCain's neighbor in the next cell whom he greatly respected, Captain Bob Craner (USAF), counseled him to go home. It was a tough decision. McCain says, "I wanted to say yes. I wanted to go home. I was tired and sick, and despite my bad attitude {toward the V}, I was afraid."[3] John could easily have justified his decision, accepted their offer, and returned home. Instead, he confronted his doubts and fears with his commitments to the honor of his family and the service of his country and fellow POWs. He would refuse early release.

In subsequent meetings, Cat continued to pressure McCain, even telling him that President Johnson had ordered him to come home.[4] John called his bluff, making it clear that he would have nothing of it. He gave his final answer to the V in a voice loud enough for fellow POWs in nearby cells to overhear: He would stay until it was his time to go home. His actions sent a message that came through loud and clear as an example to everyone in the camps, "I will return with honor."

McCain's firm stance was rewarded with almost eighteen months of abuse—the longest period of maltreatment of anyone at the

Plantation Camp.[5] Whenever he was caught communicating, he was beaten by guards. Eventually they tied him in ropes, re-breaking his arm, until he finally agreed to sign a confession of wrongdoing with apology. Because he made the right and honorable choice, John did not gain relief from isolation and abuse until treatment improved for all of us in the fall of 1969. True to his word, McCain stayed to the end. He was captured eleven days before me, and we walked out together, flying home on the same aircraft.

⑦ LESSON: CONFRONT YOUR DOUBTS AND FEARS

My own working definition of courage is that it's *doing what is right or called for in the situation, even when it does not feel safe or natural.* If your commitment (will) is strong enough, I believe you can muster the courage to make honorable choices in the face of virtually any challenge. The strength of your will is connected to your commitment to live from your deepest desires. Leading with honor is difficult; it can only be achieved when tied to such a commitment.

As you've probably concluded by now, acts of courage were common in the POW camps. In fact, it would take volumes to relate all of the stories I personally know. What about your experiences? Have you witnessed this type of courageous leadership in your organization? Do you know leaders who exhibit a similar commitment to doing what's right? You probably know several, as do I. But unfortunately, when we're honest, we have to admit that courageous leadership seems to be in short supply in many areas of our culture today.

Why is that? If these leaders in the POW camps could stand by their values in spite of humiliation, hardship, and torture, why do so many business professionals avoid making courageous choices in far less trying circumstances? If these POWs were willing to lean into the pain and take risks for their fellow prisoners, why are so few politicians willing to take risks in order to serve others? If these POWs were willing to fight so they could return with honor, why are so few leaders today willing to fight for what is honorable? Where is the courage in today's society? Where is the honor? This entire book relates to these questions about courage and honor, because almost every chapter deals in some way with the need to confront our fears and do the right thing.

We often read or hear in the media about leaders whose lack of courage reaped painful consequences. But these "spectacular" failures are just the tip of the iceberg. Doubts and fears of a much smaller magnitude have caused legions of leaders to fail in less obvious ways. Although these failures don't make the newspapers, they nevertheless can suck the energy and life out of the people and organizations they affect.

I believe that many of these less-obvious failures could be avoided if leaders learn (1) to affirm, (2) to confront, and (3) to listen. Let's examine each of these in turn.

Affirm the Value of Others

Tom, a division president in a Fortune 200 company, was a strong leader and a highly respected individual, but his reluctance to give positive feedback was hampering his leadership effectiveness. When I raised this issue, Tom said, "I don't need affirmation myself, and I don't feel comfortable giving it to others. I've tried praising people in the past, and it's always felt awkward." (As an aside, some executives I've worked with—Tom wasn't one of them—"feel" strongly that feelings have no place in the work environment. Somehow, they fail to see the contradiction!)

Perhaps Tom's discomfort was derived from a lack of affirmation in his childhood, the absence of positive role models early in his career, or his highly task-oriented, somewhat introverted temperament. Regardless of the cause, to his credit he acknowledged the problem and decided to lean into his fear. The next time Tom had an opportunity to compliment one of his staff, I helped him plan his approach. To ensure that his feedback was genuine and meaningful, we agreed that he would give very specific praise about an area where this VP had not only done well, but also knew she had done well.

The plan called for Tom to enter the VP's office smiling, take a seat when invited, and engage her in a relaxed brief conversation about her newly adopted daughter and any other light topic that came up. Then he would stretch his smile and enthusiasm to the point of becoming uncomfortable and say, "Jane, I was very pleased with the way you handled the off site retreat last week. Your planning and coordination made it a very successful and fun event. Thank you for your hard work and innovation." Then he was to excuse himself and head back to his office.

Tom's exercise in courage lifted Jane's spirits, energizing her to lead her team with more enthusiasm. It also gave Tom increased confidence in his ability to affirm his team. With this victory under his belt, he began to practice his newly acquired skill. The payoff was a boost in morale, energy, and teamwork that cascaded down through his leadership team deep into the organization. During the next two years of his incumbency, the organization thrived in spite of many challenges and substantial change.

Do you regularly affirm others? I'm not suggesting that you "flatter" them, but simply that you genuinely and consistently acknowledge their efforts and accomplishments, both large and small. Make affirmation a habit and watch what happens!

Confront Troublesome Issues and Hold People Accountable

While many leaders shy away from giving praise, even more have difficulty offering constructive criticism and holding people accountable. Uncorrected problems are like cancers; once they start growing, they get worse.

Everywhere I go, leaders tell me about underperforming employees who are sucking the energy out of leaders and teams. Often the substandard performance has been dragging on for more than a year, and nothing has been done to "call the question." Frequently I find myself having to coach leaders to initiate corrective action. It's almost as if I have to build up their courage and give them permission to do what they know they should do.

Perhaps they're afraid that if they speak frankly, people will dislike them. Or maybe they're afraid that their forthrightness will heighten tensions or cause disruptions, so they avoid "rocking the boat." Surprisingly, even the leaders who have a reputation for being "tough" often get very uncomfortable when negative emotions might be involved. Most people go to great lengths to avoid difficult conversations, controversial decisions, and unpopular actions.

Leaders who regularly avoid appropriate confrontation do a disservice to their followers, the organization, and themselves. Yes, directly engaging people and problems does entail risks, but avoiding troublesome issues creates even bigger risks. When poor performance and bad attitudes are allowed to fester, productivity will dramatically decline. When team members observe that management neglects obvious problems, they lose respect for their leadership and morale erodes.

As a workshop assignment, I once told a group of senior executives that they were each to have an honest conversation with one of their subordinates about a difficult issue that needed to be addressed. The following week, their reports to the class were enlightening. For example, one VP admitted that he had avoided dealing with a performance issue for some time. Challenged by the assignment and encouraged by the knowledge he had gained in the workshop, he confronted the employee in a strong but caring way. It turned out to be a powerful and positive conversation that cleared the air and moved the issue toward resolution.

I learned a lot about constructive confrontation from my three-time boss and long-time friend, Colonel Dick O'Grady, USAF. When I told him how much I respected the way he confronted issues rather than procrastinating, he said, "Lee, when you see a problem, you have to engage it. It usually doesn't get better over time; it gets worse." His example and counsel have helped my leadership enormously over the years. Hardly a week goes by that I don't have an opportunity to share with a client this nugget of truth, one of the many "O'Gradyisms" that have helped me grow as a leader.

Tolerating bad situations is not fair to the organization, to the employees, to you as the leader, or to the offending individual. Festering problems are unhealthy and contagious, so why put up with them? Obviously, if it's a personnel issue, consult first with Human Resources to make sure you do everything legally and in order. Then move in with a plan and take some action.[6]

It was said about General George Washington that he always "rode toward the sound of the gunfire." Fearful leaders hang back; courageous leaders develop a game plan and engage the issues. Weak leaders procrastinate, sidestep, and avoid; strong leaders confront.

Learn to Listen

Many leaders make a third mistake: they fail to listen to the ideas, opinions, and constructive feedback of others. Some go so far as to use intimidation to silence "threatening" ideas. Still others suppress ideas by dominating conversations and not allowing others to speak. These leaders may appear "macho" on the outside, but in reality their fears and insecurities send a loud message that they don't want anyone to disagree with their view of the world. Unfortunately, most of us know how exhausting and demoralizing it can be to work for a leader whose tender ego must be carefully guarded. Usually there is a graveyard outside this executive's office that's filled with the bodies of messengers who had the courage to provide honest feedback.

If you suspect that you are this type of person, let me encourage you to get a "leadership 360 assessment," so your direct reports, peers, and manager (or board of directors) can give you candid, anonymous feedback. (Now, that will take some real courage on everyone's part, won't it!) If the results indicate a problem, don't rationalize your behaviors or demonize the messengers. Engage the issues and grow into the leader you can be, the one that your followers deserve.

When the truth is courageously communicated, people and organizations flourish. But when doubts and fears hold sway, leaders avoid hard decisions and responsible actions, and instead look for a comfortable way out. At best, team energy drains away and people don't grow. Too often, fear and doubt cause bad judgment that derails the leader's influence.

The Leadership Engagement Model

Leaders who lack courage to engage problems usually veer off course in one of two directions: they will either seek to *dominate,* or they will seek to *withdraw (fight or flight; violence or silence.)*[7] Both of these counter-productive behaviors have the same root cause: fears and doubts.

I've found the Leadership Engagement Model™ depicted below to be extremely helpful for improving the cooperation and productivity of teams working cross-functionally, especially if a "silo mentality" is prevalent. It has also been beneficial for strategic partners who have competing interests.[8]

Leadership Engagement Model™		
WITHDRAW	**ENGAGE**	**DOMINATE**
Retreat	*Initiate/Involve*	*Control/Dictate*
Hide/Avoid	*Connect/Dialogue*	*Force/Bully*
Quit/Abandon	*Work Through*	*Manipulate*
Go Passive-Aggressive	*Hope/Believe*	*Blow Up*
Emotions	**Emotions**	**Emotions**
Fear	*Courage*	*Fear*
Anger	*Respect/Love*	*Anger*
Distrust	*Confidence*	*Distrust*
Shame/Guilt	*Humility*	*Pride/Hubris*

Note that the same negative emotions are listed underneath the "Withdraw" and "Dominate" behaviors. Consider how doubts and fears are connected to all of them.

For example, in most medical communities a natural tension exists between the hospital and the physicians and clinics that use the hospital. Typically, one party tries to *dominate* to get its way, which in turn causes the other party to become distrustful and combative. Eventually, emotions can get so raw that one party *withdraws,* or they both do. To halt this vicious cycle, the two sides need to courageously commit to *engage* in productive dialog, identify common goals, and implement agreed-upon solutions. Meaningful engagement occurs when each party fights for its ideas in a healthy, constructive way, while still being open to the ideas of others. This type of dialog is evidence of humility, courage, and confidence.

Doubts and fears are normal. You can't avoid them, but you can manage them. You can choose to override your feelings and do the right thing. You can choose to lean into the pain for the good of others and yourself. Like the men in the POW camps you've read about, you can choose to be a strong leader by being courageous.

Foot Stomper: Authentic leaders develop courage as an act of will. Choose today to do what you know to be right, even when it feels unnatural or unsafe. Trust yourself, honor your values, lean into your pain, and intentionally *engage* issues with strength and humility, despite your fears.

⑦ Coaching: CONFRONT YOUR DOUBTS AND FEARS

As in every area of leadership development, step one is awareness. The questions below may help you identify ways in which you can develop more courage.

1. What type(s) of courage might you be lacking: physical courage, professional or political courage, reputational courage, financial courage, personal and emotional courage, relational courage?

   For example, with respect to relational courage, does fear keep you from holding others accountable at work? Do you shy away from setting boundaries with others? Do you lack the personal and emotional courage to give and receive constructive feedback?

2. In what specific situations might you be dominating or withdrawing (e.g., by attacking or procrastinating) when you should be engaging?

3. What choices do you need to make to engage issues you have been avoiding?

Note: To download an expanded version of these coaching questions for writing your responses, visit LeadingWithHonor.com/Book.

---

[1] John M. McGrath, *Prisoner of War: Six Years in Hanoi*. (Annapolis, MD: Naval Institute Press, 1975) 45.

[2] Hearing the turnkey's key rattle outside the cell other than at normal mealtimes or bucket-emptying times set off an emotional alarm that something bad was about to happen.

[3] John S. McCain and Mark Salter, *Faith of My Fathers*. (New York, NY: Random House, 1999) 235.

[4] John Hubbell, *POW: A Definitive History of the American Prisoner-of-War Experience in Vietnam, 1964-1973*. (New York, NY: The Readers Digest Press, 1976) 452.

[5] Zalin Grant, "John McCain, How the POWs Fought Back," *US News & World Report*, May 14, 1973, 49-51.

[6] See these books for help on holding others accountable: *Crucial Confrontations* by Kerry Patterson, Joseph Grenny, Ron McMillan, and Al Switzler. *Conversations* by Susan Scott.

[7] The book *Crucial Conversations* (Kerry Patterson, Joseph Grenny, Ron McMillan, and Al Switzler) gives many tips on how to engage effectively and uses the terms "silence" and "violence" to describe withdrawing and dominating behaviors.

[8] The Leadership Engagement Model is available as a small card for download or purchase at www.LeadingWithHonor.com/Courage.

Chapter 5

FIGHT TO WIN

★

*"Winning isn't everything,
but the will to win is everything."*

Vince Lombardi

By the time Operation Rolling Thunder air campaign over North Vietnam began in the spring of 1965, Hanoi and Haiphong were the most highly defended areas in the world. More than 70 percent of American POWs during the war were pilots and crew members shot down in that campaign. Air Force Lt Col Robbie Risner and Navy Commanders Jeremiah Denton and Jim Stockdale were among the first casualties. These squadron commanders already had been recognized as exceptional leaders prior to their capture. As survivors of the Great Depression and World War II, they were among the youngest members of what Tom Brokaw called "The Greatest Generation." Bright, well-educated, courageous, strong-willed, and as tough as nails, these three were men of honor to whom we all looked for guidance and inspiration.

The North Vietnamese constantly sought to use senior POWs as propaganda tools in staged press conferences. Korean War Ace[1] Robbie Risner, our camp SRO during the early days, was a prime target for exploitation. Prior to parading Risner before a "peace delegation," the V tortured him and prepped him on how to answer reporters' questions. Risner infuriated his captors during the press conference by refusing to regurgitate the party line. Aware that they had promised to give a journalist access to two family photographs he had received from home, he tore up the photos, hid them in the waste bucket, and refused to disclose their location. Because the V badly wanted the photos for propaganda purposes and did not want to lose face with the journalist, they frantically searched his cell for them, but to no avail. The one place they didn't look was at the bottom of that pail of human excrement.

In an effort to force him to produce the photos, the guards severely beat Robbie and put him through the rope torture. The "ropes," or "pretzel" as it was sometimes called, was a terrifying and brutal method for breaking POWs. After the prisoner's legs were tied together, his arms were laced tightly behind his back until the elbows touched and the shoulders were virtually pulled out of joint. Then the torturer would push the bound arms up and over the head, while applying pressure with a knee to the victim's back, as shown in the graphic below.

The "Ropes" or "Pretzel" Torture[2]
Drawing by former POW Mike McGrath

During torture, the circulation is cut off and the limbs go to sleep, but the joint pain continues to increase as the ligaments and muscles tear. When the ropes are finally removed, circulation surges back into the "dead" limbs, causing excruciating pain.

When the V eventually learned what Risner had done with the photos, they furiously inflicted more torture until Robbie agreed to sign a confession and an apology for committing "grave crimes." Under such severe torture, no POW could resist signing these forced statements. We took some comfort in the fact that they invariably sounded phony, because they were dictated by the V using awkward sentence structure and expressions that no American would use. Sometimes they were so ridiculous they made the V look foolish.

After torture, the guards boarded up the window in Risner's cell, making it so dark he couldn't see the walls. Robbie had never been afraid of the dark, but he immediately began to have panic attacks. In later describing this episode he said, "It was as if I had an animal on my back. Absolute panic had set in. The fact that I could not control this thing driving me caused me to be even more panic-stricken...sheer desolation permeated the miserable dark cell I lived in twenty-four hours a day."[3]

Risner's only relief was to keep moving and praying. He would walk around his cell—often covering as many as twenty miles a day—and do pushups and sit-ups, until he was exhausted enough to fall asleep. If he awakened during the night, he had to resume exercising until he was again exhausted enough to sleep. It was a maddening existence. At times he wanted to scream, but since that would bring more torture, he would hide under his mosquito net, stuff something in his mouth, wrap his blanket around his head, and "just holler" until the anxiety eased. Often he had to talk himself into making it through one more minute and then one more minute. As he put it, "I literally lived one minute at a time."[4]

After ten months of darkness, the night finally passed. In June 1968, the V moved Robbie into the Golden Nugget section of Little Vegas. From our cell about forty feet away, we heard him moaning and screaming in nightmares throughout that first night. The next day, when Robbie's shutters were opened, I saw his tired but smiling face for the first time. During siesta, while the guards were generally less alert, Risner and I made contact. Over the next few days, he shared his story and basic guidance by writing with his index finger on his open palm, one letter of the alphabet at a time. It was clear that he had a lot of fight left in him. His courage served as inspiration for the rest of us in the months and years ahead.

Facing similar propaganda exploitation, CDR Jeremiah Denton endured excruciating torture before finally agreeing to go before the propaganda cameras. Prior to filming, his captors prepped him for several days on what he was supposed to say about America's "cruel and oppressive war." But in the press conference, Denton, at risk of his life, departed from the party-line script and said, "… whatever my government is doing, I agree with it, and I will support it as long as I live."

The V were stunned. Not wanting to lose face with the reporters, however, they allowed Denton to continue answering questions about the daily camp routine. They were unaware that as the cameras rolled, he was blinking his eyes in Morse code: $T - O - R - T - U - R - E$.[5] The payoff was huge. When the video of the interview went public, it was the first time the U.S. government had accurate information about the treatment of POWs.

Angered by Denton's departure from the script, but still unaware of his encoded communication, the V displayed their trophy at another staged press conference two weeks later. This time Denton stood up while on camera and walked out. The consequences were severe. The V put Denton in the rope torture and then beat him until he was unconscious.[6]

Denton's courage is all the more exemplary when one considers that he knew that this type of torture awaited him if he defied his captors.[7] During his seven and a half years in captivity, he never hesitated to provide leadership when he was the SRO of a cellblock or camp. Although that made him a prime target for abuse and exploitation by the enemy, he steadfastly pushed himself and the enemy to the limit. He deliberately kept the torture team occupied, so they would have less time to harass his fellow POWs. Denton's will to win was motivated by his strong sense of personal and professional commitment, undergirded by his deep faith in God.

By the time Navy CDR James Bond Stockdale was shot down and captured, two months after Denton, he had already established a reputation as an outstanding aviator, with more than two hundred combat missions to his credit. A year earlier, he had been the first man on the scene at the Gulf of Tonkin incident, the still-controversial event that landed Navy LT Everett (Ev) Alvarez in Hanoi, where he led a lonely six-month existence until other American POWs began to arrive.[8]

Stockdale was a twentieth-century Renaissance man. As a teenager, he played piano, acted in leading roles in his high school drama club, and was a stalwart on the football team. After graduating from the U. S. Naval Academy, he became one of the Navy's top test pilots. Later the Navy sent him to postgraduate school to earn a master's degree in international relations at Stanford University, where he became a dedicated student of the classics. The faculty encouraged him to pursue a doctorate degree, but he decided to return to his first love as a fighter pilot. Stockdale's keen understanding of Marxism and his appreciation for the classics, especially Stoicism, equipped him well for his role as a POW leader.

When his plane was shot down over North Vietnam, Stockdale sustained a broken back during ejection. Following his capture, the civilian populace severely beat him, breaking his leg and dislocating his shoulder. A medic was about to amputate his leg, but Stockdale returned to consciousness just in time to convince him to apply a cast. In spite of his injuries, the V tortured him in the months ahead, even kicking and yanking his dangling limbs to increase the pain.

CDR Stockdale, as SRO in Little Vegas, helped instill a strong and unified culture in the camps that raised morale and increased POW resistance. The V began a purge, torturing men viciously to find out who was responsible.[9] Stockdale was eventually exposed and moved to the torture chambers, where he underwent severe beatings, torture cuffs,[10] and the ropes, until he finally agreed to sign a "confession."

Because Stockdale was such a determined resistor and the senior ranking naval officer in the camps, the enemy constantly targeted him for exploitation. In early 1968, after considerable torture, they arranged for him to perform as an actor in a propaganda film. Recognizing what they were up to, Stockdale used the razor they had given him for shaving his beard to cut his hair into a reverse Mohawk. In the process, he deliberately sliced his scalp so that it bled profusely. Not to be denied, the V brought their "actor" a hat to wear for the filming. Left alone in the interrogation room, Stockdale grabbed a wooden stool and beat his face until it was a bloody pulp, rendering himself unusable for the filming.[11]

CDR Stockdale went through torture periodically for the next three years. During his seven-and-a-half years of captivity, he spent more than four years in solitary confinement, two of which were in the infamous "Alcatraz Prison," yet he maintained his fighting spirit. The severe injuries Stockdale suffered during ejection from his aircraft and subsequent capture were never adequately treated; he walked with a severe limp for the rest of his life. Ever the Stoic, however, he was mentally well prepared for his disability and often *encouraged* himself with the words of his favorite Stoic, Epictetus: "Lameness is an impediment to the leg but not to the will." Like Risner, Denton, and many other exemplary leaders in the POW camps, Stockdale understood that a person who won't quit can't be beaten.

⑦ LESSON: FIGHT TO WIN

Life itself is a fight at virtually every turn. To win in sports, the athlete must fight against the limitations of the body and the efforts of the competition. To win the new job, the candidate must fight for the interview and for the offer. To win at home, the spouse or parent must fight against the natural human traits of selfishness and pride. Even to win at a simple game of chess or bridge or golf, the player must fight with tenacious concentration.

Nothing worthwhile in life comes easily. Some days you will feel good, and some days you won't. But regardless of feelings and circumstances, you must make up your mind to persevere. If you want to be victorious, you must decide in advance to fight to win. That's what the senior leaders did. They went first, and they set the bar very high.

The battles in your organization are probably less intense than those that took place in the POW camps, but they can be daunting nevertheless. If you're a business leader, for example, you must constantly fight to increase revenues, develop new products, attract new employees, complete projects on time, promote teamwork, ensure quality, confront employees who are underperforming, and achieve a host of other important goals. In fact, you must in a very real sense fight for the survival of your organization every day. What's more, you must continually fight to uphold your personal and professional commitments and values, in spite of fears, doubts, and temptations to compromise. That requires the same kind of tenacity POW leaders exhibited.

As a kid, we used to play pickup games of basketball and touch football. The two best players would take turns choosing the players they wanted on their team. The smart leaders didn't always select the players with the most natural talent. They picked the ones who had the greatest desire to win, who had what we call "fire in their belly." So it is with life. Talent, education, charisma, and good looks will only get you so far. To win in life, you must want to win and you must fight to win.

Find Your Drive for Success

In the business context, highly motivated people are said to have "drive," or perhaps a "pioneering spirit." They are willing and even eager to step out into uncharted territories, launch new initiatives, take on the most challenging tasks, and pursue lofty goals. Leaders with drive inspire, push, persuade, direct, and challenge others to take the actions that are required to attain the goals that are desired.

Leaders who are driven to win in every undertaking typically manifest the positive personality traits of assertiveness, initiative, desire for achievement, persistence, and ambition. These are good qualities. Leaders with strong drive get things done. But as in other areas of life, too much of a good thing can be counterproductive. When all of these traits are in play without an awareness and concern for the capabilities and needs of others, watch out! A "driven" leader who is inordinately focused on results can push others into "burnout" rather quickly. That's not healthy for the organization or for the individuals involved.

Other personality styles focus their drive on a more limited set of goals. For example, some athletes are extremely competitive when engaging in their sport, but are not so driven in other areas. I witnessed this a few years ago while providing career coaching to professional athletes who were approaching retirement. One All-Pro NFL football player was a fierce competitor on the field, but he was relaxed and somewhat laid back when engaged in other activities. His drive to win centered on his passion for the game. It was fueled by his desire to be the best in his field.

On another consulting assignment where I was asked to assess the personality traits of various store managers, I encountered one leader who measured quite low in the area of drive. She was very successful on the job, however, so we dug deeper. It turned out that her drive came from a strong motivation in two seemingly unrelated areas: to provide great customer service and to creatively present innovative products and services.

In some individuals this pioneering drive is a dominant personality trait that affects broad areas of their lives; these people will fight to win at every undertaking. Others who might be world-class performers in their profession might have that same kind of fight in only a few endeavors; it's just the way they are wired. Good leaders have a knack for identifying the sources of each individual's unique drive to win, and then tapping into it for the benefit of the organization and the individual.

Fight for Win-Win Outcomes

Fighter pilots by nature are competitive. They have to be, because they're trained to engage in life-and-death combat. But in most work environments, ultra-high competitiveness is counterproductive. "Fighting" needs to fit the environment and the situation. In all organizations, striving to win at the expense of others is a losing proposition. An insatiable need to always be right and win every argument can derail relationships and even careers.

On several occasions I've been asked to coach executives who were outstanding in almost every way, except they had excessive drive. Some were so dominant they could not cooperate with their teammates, and at times they even bucked their boss. They made a habit of turning discussions about minor issues into arguments. These individuals were good people with good intentions, but they could not see that their behaviors were out of balance. My job was to help them become aware in the moment of the situational dynamics, so they could then learn to manage their interactions in a successful way.

I'll never forget one individual who called to tell me about his success. He said that after a staff meeting one of his peers came to him and asked him if he was feeling okay. He replied, "Sure, why do you ask?" His peer responded, "You were not yourself today in the meeting. You were quieter than usual and didn't get into any arguments." My client was quite proud of his achievements, and so was I. He didn't reinvent himself, but he did learn to manage his natural drive to win. His career has continued upward, and he now manages a large segment of a Fortune 100 company.

Drive is a helpful quality, but like most other leadership traits, it can be powered by inappropriate motivations. When individuals allow unbridled ambition, greed, or other unhealthy needs to fuel their desire to win, the results are almost invariably destructive for that person and for the organization. Legitimate needs and worthwhile goals are seldom met when "steamroller" methods are used to pursue selfish desires.

When fighting to win, know when to fight. Sometimes you have to withdraw from the battle for a while. As POWs, there came a time during torture when it was evident we could not beat them at their game. We had to find a different approach for achieving our goals. When you know for sure you can't win, it's probably time to quit doing what you're doing and rethink your strategy. But before throwing in the towel, check with your teammates, your mentor, or others you trust to get their counsel. And, keep in mind the "First Law of Holes: When you're in one, stop digging!"[12]

Outstanding leaders seek to understand the true nature of their own motivations and the motivations of those they lead, and then they make adjustments as necessary. As Jim Collins points out in his best selling book *Good to Great*, the best leaders are typically highly competitive, but they harness that competitiveness for the good of the organization, not to boost their own egos.

Foot Stomper: Successful leaders believe in their mission and fight to carry it out successfully. They don't quit; they expect to win; they take others with them; and they give others the credit.

⑦ Coaching: FIGHT TO WIN

Drive (energy to overcome obstacles) can come from a variety of sources. Having a clear understanding of your deepest motivations provides significant self-awareness and enables you to manage and coach yourself. Reflect on these questions to gain more insights about the sources and effects of your drive.

1. **What are the primary sources of your drive?**
   (Check all that strongly apply.)

   - Desire to achieve goals
   - Desire to excel
   - Desire to do my best
   - Desire to be number one
   - Desire to serve others
   - Desire to honor God
   - Desire for money
   - Desire for recognition
   - Desire to please others

   - Desire for power
   - Passion for what I'm doing
   - Challenge of competing
   - Fear of failure
   - Thrill of success
   - Love of the "game"
   - Love of adventure
   - Drive to look good
   - Other sources of drive…

2. **Are your drive and ambition focused on helping the team succeed?** If your drive is too intense or too weak, in what ways might you be hurting the team? How could you find out how you are affecting others? Will you make an effort to find out?

3. **Does your drive to win interfere with your relationships?** Do you tend to "beat people down" or "lift them up"? How can you learn about how you influence the motivations and confidence of others?

Note: To download an expanded version of these coaching questions for writing your responses, visit LeadingWithHonor.com/Book.

---

[1] Lt Col Risner had been the squadron commander for five of the early POWs, including Majors Larry Guarino, Ron Byrne, and Ray Merritt, and Captains Smitty Harris and Wes Schierman.

[2] John M. McGrath, *Prisoner of War: Six Years in Hanoi.* (Annapolis, MD: Naval Institute Press, 1975) 79.

[3] Robinson Risner, *The Passing of the Night.* (Old Saybrook, CT: Konecky & Konecky, 1973) 178-179.

[4] Risner, 180.

[5] A video of the press conference showing Denton blinking T-O-R-T-U-R-E is available at http://www.youtube.com/watch?v=BgelmcOdS38 (accessed May 15, 2010).

[6] Denton was awarded the Navy Cross for courage and gallantry as a POW. This medal is the highest award given by the Navy.

[7] Denton documented his POW experience not long after our release in a book appropriately titled *When Hell Was in Session.* In 1979, the book was made into a movie with actor Hal Holbrook playing Denton. Eva Marie Saint played his courageous wife Jane, who soldiered on at home, rearing seven children while her husband was a POW for seven and a half years.

[8] American warships patrolling the Gulf of Tonkin reported radar contact with what was believed to be enemy gunboats. President Johnson used this event to launch attacks on North Vietnamese targets.

[9] This was the same purge (Stockdale Purge) that made it so difficult for us to communicate when we arrived in Little Vegas in the fall of 1967. The purge was so effective that we did not know much of the camp history until the long-term POWs moved in next door at Son Tay in November 1968.

[10] Torture cuffs were handcuffs that could be ratcheted down tighter and tighter until they cut off circulation, even cut through the skin into the muscle. On some men, they cut deep enough to expose bone.

[11] Stockdale was awarded the Congressional Medal of Honor for his heroism in the North Vietnamese prisons.

[12] Denis Healey, *"Brainy Quotes,"* http://www.brainyquote.com/quotes/authors/d/denis_healey.html (accessed November 14, 2010).

Chapter 6

BOUNCE BACK

"If you can force your heart and nerve and sinew
to serve your turn long after they are gone,
and so hold on when there is nothing in you
except the Will which says to them:
'Hold on!'... Yours is the Earth
and everything that's in it,..."

Rudyard Kipling[1]

The anguish of the first few months of captivity was unrelenting. We were cold and hungry every day. Interrogators repeatedly threatened to try us as war criminals, and guards were constantly banging on our doors telling us to "keep quiet." The overhanging threat of torture further depressed our spirits. When the siren went off for bombing raids over Hanoi—as many as ten times a night—the V made us get up, crawl under the wooden beds, and lay on the cold, nasty floor. The concussions from nearby bombs sometimes rattled the prison doors, but our biggest concern from the air raids was gravity. What goes up must come down, and the communist gunners were filling the sky with iron from their surface to air missiles (SAMs) and huge 85mm and 100mm antiaircraft artillery.

Traumatic stress invaded my sleep. I regularly dreamed that I was fighting an endless procession of Vietnamese communist soldiers. When I ran out of ammo for my M-16 rifles and pistols, I'd grab one of their AK-47s and continue shooting. Miraculously, I could bring down twenty to fifty V without getting hit, and then I'd take out five or ten more in hand-to-hand combat. Eventually, I was too exhausted to keep fighting, and one of them would get me. As I lay dying, I would force myself to realize it was a dream and wake up. We were not flying combat any more, but our battle against the enemy continued both day and night. It was a life-and-death struggle in which even the simplest of events could have serious repercussions. With little control over our daily existence, we desperately searched for anchor points to hang on.

Over time we somewhat adapted to the environment, and POW life became our "normal" life. Like someone living with a disease or losing a loved one, you learn to carry on the best you can. Without any conscious awareness or effort, my mind gained enough psychological and emotional freedom to allow my sense of humor to resurface. I still remember the first time I was able to laugh, about three months after we arrived in Hanoi.

The nightly gong had rung, signaling time to go to bed. As we were about to turn in, cellmate Jim Warner made a wry comment about the politics of the war that was cleverly intended to draw the ire of LtCol Minter and further expose his sympathy for the enemy. Recognizing what he was doing, I rolled my eyes and quipped, "Jim, you're just trolling, aren't you?"

Instantly the dam broke. Jim and I fell into uncontrollable laughter, to the point of both tears and sweat. It was wonderful therapy that freed us at least briefly from the shackles of fear and worry. From that point forward, we intentionally looked for every opportunity to laugh, even in the direst situations. We'd often take enormous risks just to pass along a funny story or a new joke, with full realization that laughing out loud could land us in solitary…or worse.

We began to find humor even in the nightly propaganda broadcasts of Hanoi Hannah. For instance, at that time the state of Illinois was abbreviated "Ill." Hanoi Hannah provided us with a good chuckle by mispronouncing Chicago, Ill, as "Cheek-a-go-3." Another time, she attempted to substantiate a propaganda assertion by quoting no less of an authority than "a middle-aged lady from Detroit." Thereafter, whenever any of us was questioned about the veracity of a statement we had made, we would say, "It has to be true; I heard it from a middle-aged lady from Detroit."

Captain Bob "Percy" Purcell (USAF) was a stereotypical wild-and-woolly fighter pilot with a gallows humor that knew no bounds.

In July 1966, camp guards marched Percy and about fifty other POWs in a propaganda parade through downtown Hanoi. Right away it became clear that this was going to be a nasty pep rally to generate hate. Communist Party cadre (operatives) walked alongside, screaming invectives through bullhorns to incite the gathering crowd. The mob began to scream, "Kowtow!" demanding that the POWs drop their heads in shame. Some reached past the guards to throw punches. Handcuffed by twos and helpless, the Americans were in danger of serious injury, if not death. Then, in the midst of this powder keg of chaos, Percy began singing in a loud voice, "I love a parade! I love a parade!"

A guard nicknamed "Dum Dum" grabbed Percy by the neck and tried to bend his head to make him bow. Percy laughed, kept his head high, and began carrying the guard along with him. It's hard to describe how much this humorous act of brave defiance lifted POW spirits in the midst of a nightmarish situation. This story was told and retold in the camps for years. Even today, former POWs enjoy sharing stories of Percy's courageous and humorous act of defiance.

Percy was on the receiving end of humorous incidents, too. A few months after his capture, his old squadron mate, Captain Wes Schierman, joined him at the Hanoi Hilton. "Back home you've been declared killed in action," Wes informed Percy, "so don't expect me to go to your funeral. I've already attended your memorial service!"

The scientific and medical communities increasingly report how humor can relieve stress and lighten depression. In the POW camps, laughter proved to be crucial for our survival. It provided a ray of light and gave us hope that this long period of darkness would someday pass.

As you have already heard, many men sustained serious wounds during their high-speed bailouts and from subsequent abuse and torture. Other POWs struggled with illnesses and infections that persisted for years due to poor or non-existent medical care. Sadly, not all of the sick and wounded POWs came home, but considering the circumstances, it's quite amazing that most did.

Air Force Captain Jeff Ellis (a good friend, but not related) incurred a compound fracture that shattered his leg during ejection from his F-105. The V straightened it and wired the remaining solid bones back together, but it was permanently two inches shorter than the other. For the duration of his captivity, small pieces of bone occasionally extruded from his leg, and fluids regularly drained from it. But Jeff never complained; he endured the suffering, served with distinction, and returned home to continue his flying career. When I retired from the Air Force more than twenty years after we were captured, it was a great honor to salute my commander, Brig Gen Jeff Ellis, as he presided over the ceremony.

The year before I arrived, most of the POWs living at the Briarpatch, a camp near the mountains outside Hanoi, were stricken with beriberi.[2] Captains Chuck Boyd and Smitty Harris had to walk on the cold floor of their cell until their feet were numb enough to allow them to sleep for a while without pain. When the diet and treatment improved, they were able to bounce back. Boyd lost his pilot's vision as a result of the disease, but it did not stop him from being the only Vietnam POW to reach the rank of four-star general. Smitty retired as a colonel, earned a law degree, managed a large law firm, and eventually retired again. He can still score his age in golf.

Cellmate Wes Schierman suffered with an illness similar to asthma. It flared up so badly when the weather was cold and damp that we feared for his life. As he wheezed, coughed, and gasped through the night, we prayed that he would survive until daylight, when his condition usually improved. Wes's persistence and resilience inspired us to endure our hardships. After he returned to the States, he completely recovered and passed the FAA flight physical. Northwest Airlines recalled him as a pilot, even honoring his seniority. Wes captained commercial airliners for many years, until he reached mandatory retirement age.

LCDR John McCain and Major Bud Day endured some of the most severe wounds of all POWs, but the care of a cellmate enabled them to hold on until their health improved enough to care for each other. They kept the faith that a better day was coming. Over time their bodies began to recover from the initial injuries sustained during ejection, capture, and torture. Both had permanent damage to bone structure, which to this day prevents them from fully using their arms. Nevertheless, at the time of this writing, Day, in his eighties, is practicing law, and McCain, in his seventies, is serving as a U.S. Senator from Arizona.

In November 1970, the V suddenly moved more than two hundred of us from Camp Faith back to the Hanoi Hilton. We had no idea why, until we learned from some newly captured POWs that a U.S. Special Forces team had raided the Son Tay camp, seeking to free us. Unfortunately, we had been moved away from Son Tay to open Camp Faith a few months earlier.[3]

The initial excitement about this raid soon withered. We realized that such a dangerous, high-risk mission would not have been undertaken if the end of the war was in sight. The morale of a few men began to plummet. Fortunately, at that time each cell held forty to sixty POWs, so we were able to draw strength from each other.

We were definitely a band of brothers, and we leaned on each other in difficult times. Fellow POW Ted Stier put it this way: "When people ask me how I was able to endure for all those years, I reply that I derived most of my strength from other POWs, especially the 'old heads' who were captured in '65 and '66. If I found that I was feeling sorry for myself or I was having a bad day—really down in the dumps—I could count on them to listen to my problems and give me words of encouragement or greet me with a cheerful face."[4]

With no books, TV, magazines, newspapers, or other sources of information or entertainment, we were our sole source of learning, encouragement, and inspiration. We started weekly ecumenical church services featuring a variety of speakers recruited by the designated program manager.

I will always remember a message on resilience one cold and dreary Sunday shortly after we moved back to the Hanoi Hilton. Air Force Captain Jon Reynolds, an F-105 pilot and a reserved Philadelphia Episcopalian, stepped up on the elevated concrete sleeping slab in the center of the room to address the group. Jon had been seriously injured when he ejected. He could not chew for months due to a broken jaw.

Both arms were broken above the elbows, so they hung by his side like a rag doll. Through self-therapy over a long period, Jon's jaw healed and his arms recovered, eventually to the point where he could do one-arm pushups.

This tough warrior, whom we all respected for the suffering he had endured, challenged us to let go of our self-pity and consider our blessings. Pointing out that we had survived the difficult years and that the treatment was better now, he told us to look around the room and see that we still had our health. He reminded us we were the fortunate ones who were still alive. We had bounced back in the past, and we could do it again if we kept the faith. We had the hope of returning home to freedom, our families, our beloved country, and a bright future.[5] It was the right message by the right person at the right time. We were all uplifted; one man who was contemplating suicide snapped back and eventually returned home with honor.

As bad as our situation was, we were alive and we could fight for our survival. Back home, however, our families didn't even know if we were dead or alive. All they could do was wait and pray. To make matters worse, the defense and veterans agencies were not prepared to respond effectively to POW/MIA families. Further compounding their sense of helplessness, U.S. Government officials told these families to keep quiet. Decision makers were reluctant to press the North Vietnamese about the POW situation for fear of endangering our lives.

Louise Harris, wife of Capt "Smitty" Harris, was the first MIA wife to buck the system. Very early in the war she led the charge to convince the Air Force, the VA, and other agencies to become more proactive in helping POW/MIA families resolve issues related to receipt of pay, approval of home loans, and other practical difficulties resulting from the loss of their husbands. Louise went to the top, personally explaining the issues to the Secretary of the Air Force and Senator John Stennis, Chairman of the Senate Armed Services Committee. This soft-spoken lady from Mississippi explained in her genteel "steel magnolia" way how unreasonable decisions, inflexible bureaucratic barriers, and unclear policies of government agencies were making matters worse.[6]

The agencies responded with more realistic, family-friendly policies.

Sybil Stockdale (wife of CDR Stockdale), Ann Purcell (wife of Lt Col Ben Purcell), Doris Day (wife of Maj Bud Day), and Elaine Grubb (wife of MIA Capt Wilmer Grubb) banded together with other family members to launch the National League of POW/MIA Families. They lobbied hard in meetings with the brass, including Secretary of State Kissinger and President Nixon. They made their points, and aided by MIA wife Carol Hanson Hickerson's boldness in speaking about our plight, brought a change to Department of Defense's "keep quiet" policy on POW/MIA issues.

Students at Commerce High School wearing POW/MIA bracelets bearing the name and shoot down date of the author.

The League quickly mobilized public opinion across the United States by organizing local chapters to engage POW/MIA families and their friends within their communities. Special programs were held at churches, schools, and college and professional sporting events to remember and support the POW/MIA cause. Patriots across the nation began wearing POW/MIA name bracelets[7], which linked each wearer in a tangible and emotional way with a specific serviceman who was captured or missing.

The League used this momentum to launch a letter-writing campaign aimed at communist diplomats at the stalled Paris peace talks. The total public relations effort had the important effect of slamming the communists for our treatment.

The dedicated support of business icon and national patriot H. Ross Perot helped their cause, and in doing so helped ours. Perot used his influence and wealth to support the League's PR campaign, and he provided air transportation and traveling expenses for its leaders. As part of a strategy put together by Dallas TV personality Murphy Martin, Perot sponsored trips by delegations of wives and family members to the Paris peace talks, where POW wife Phyllis Galanti and others confronted the communist delegation about the treatment of POWs. Perot also chartered airplanes to fly Christmas presents to POWs in Hanoi, but when they got to Thailand, the communists denied them entry. This made the V look bad and raised the plight of the POWs in the eyes of world citizens. It was vital support we needed.

Sybil Stockdale moved to Washington, DC, to take a full-time role as chairman of the National League of POW/MIA Families. As the years wore on, the stress of the League's fight and the anxiety and loneliness of being a POW wife began to wear her down. In addition to waging political battles and wrestling for the minds and hearts of the politicians and bureaucrats in Washington, she was raising four children in the tumultuous '60s and struggling with serious financial challenges as a single mom. Her responsibilities and struggles eventually overwhelmed her. One day after the kids were off to school, she crawled back into bed and pulled the covers over her head. The debilitating grip of depression was strangling her spirit.

Sybil's doctor had encouraged her to see a psychotherapist. But as she later related, "Every fiber of my New England body reverberated with the shock of such a suggestion.... How in the name of God could

I justify being such a weakling that I needed psychiatric help? Only those who caved in to self-pity and self-indulgence caved in and went to psychiatrists.... My body wouldn't do what my mind told it to do..... It stayed in bed hiding its head under the pillow, trying to shut the world out."[8]

As Sybil lay there talking with herself, she came to the conclusion that she could not quit. She had a duty to continue the battle, but she needed help. Leaning into the pain of her pride, she called her doctor for a referral to a therapist. It took several tries to find the right professional, but his therapy and friendship helped her bounce back. Sybil's optimism and spunk returned; she carried on with her duties in a remarkable way. Her leadership made a tremendous difference, not only for POW/MIA wives and families, but also for those of us in the camps who were clinging to life.

The resilience of these wives, families, and supporters was vital to our resilience as POWs. The League's efforts attacked the North Vietnamese at their most vulnerable point: public opinion. The campaign exposed North Vietnam's inhumane policies, making them look bad in the eyes of American citizens, and indeed the world. That undermined the communist strategy of winning over the minds and hearts of the American people; they were compelled to improve our treatment.

Beginning in the fall of 1969, most of the torture abruptly stopped. We began to receive more food and fresh air, and we were allowed to communicate more openly with others. Most of us wrote our first six-line letter home in early 1970. By that time, I had been in captivity more than two years; some had been there for four.

Clearly, the POW/MIA movement in the states played an important role in our survival and well-being, and it played perfectly into the hands of fate. The death of Ho Chi Minh in September of 1969 came just as the effects of the POW/MIA campaign back home were beginning to tarnish the image of the North Vietnamese communists. The change in leadership gave the V a perfect opportunity to do a dialectic dance in policy. Our care became more important to them; amazingly, they even quit referring to us as "creeminals."

The story of the families who bounced back from their personal losses to help each other and the POWs is a remarkable lesson in resilience. It also highlights the importance of leadership. A just cause initiated and executed by dedicated leaders is a powerful force for change.

As we sat in our cells and the years passed by, we would often discuss what it would be like to return home. We speculated that people would be curious about how we had endured for so long. In fact, even we were amazed at our resilience.

After our release, indeed many people did ask, "How did you hold on for so long and come home so physically and mentally healthy?" My short answer is that the human body, mind, and spirit can endure and overcome far more than one might expect. When we're beaten down, the physical body and the human psyche have an amazing ability to persevere. A strong will and a positive outlook, undergirded by an unwavering commitment to duty, can overcome enormous hardships. Add to that the support of others and a strong spiritual faith, and you have the fundamental formula for bouncing back.

⑦ LESSON: BOUNCE BACK

The dictionary defines resilience as 1. *the power or ability to return to the original form, position, etc., after being bent, compressed, or stretched; elasticity,* 2. *The ability to recover readily from illness, depression, adversity, or the like; buoyancy.*[9] Leaders especially need resilience to overcome the struggles and setbacks that invariably come with the role. They must be able to draw on a deep reservoir of mental and emotional strength built on a foundation of attributes and competencies like those outlined in this book.

Resilience is an American Tradition

We can learn a lot about resiliency from General George Washington, commander of the Continental Army.[10] In the winter of 1777-78 at Valley Forge, Washington inspired an army of more than ten thousand poorly trained, half-starved citizen-soldiers to endure the coldest weather of the entire war. Many had no shoes, coat, or blanket, and would have much preferred to quit and return home. At the same time, Washington was fighting off a political insurrection by two generals and trying to shore up the waning support of a Congress that had little understanding of the struggles Washington's army was facing.

Washington bounced back from that disastrous winter, overcoming political backstabbing, the treason of his close friend Benedict Arnold, and numerous defeats at the hand of the best-trained and best-equipped army in the world. He husbanded his resources, conducting only harassment raids, until the situation was favorable for a major battle. That opportunity came when British General Cornwallis, worn down by the years of fighting, moved into a defensive position at Yorktown.

If anyone had a right to rest, it was Washington. But upon learning that his French Navy allies were sailing to Chesapeake Bay, he decided to surround the British for one decisive encounter. Bouncing back from near exhaustion, he and his army marched five hundred miles from Rhode Island to Virginia and fought the battle that won the war. The key to that victory was not Washington's cleverness, or even his courage, but his resilience.

Duty

There were numerous reasons we POWs were able to resist, endure torture, and bounce back; many of them relate to our sense of duty. Duty, the indispensable attribute taught in virtually every leadership training program[11], is built on a foundation of faithfulness, character, and commitment.

We were resilient because we were faithfully committed to each other and to our country. Back at home, Sybil Stockdale's sense of duty as a wife, mother, and chairman of the League of POW/MIA families empowered her to bounce back. My parents, Molene and Leon, and my brother, Robert, and his wife, Pat, took it as their duty to support me and other POW/MIAs. They made speeches, wrote letters, gave interviews, and worked unceasingly, doing everything possible to engage our community, and indeed all Northeast Georgia, in our cause.

Resilience empowered by duty is vital to all organizational success. It takes many different forms in response to various needs. In the face of an economic slump or competitive challenge, a business leader may have to struggle tenaciously for profitability, and even survival. An organizational layoff may force the remaining employees to persevere under a heavier workload. A manager with an unprofessional boss may have to shield other employees from irrational decisions and hostile behaviors, while still remaining loyal.

One COO with whom I worked had to navigate through a professional minefield. He wanted to remain completely loyal to his boss, but he found himself fighting with his boss about questionable decisions that were undermining the foundation of the organization and draining energy from the leadership team. Eventually, however, the CEO's poor judgment crossed the line in several areas, resulting in his removal.

Because this COO had exhibited such a strong sense of duty and loyalty throughout this period, the organization continued to perform at a high level during a very stressful time. As is often the case, the resilience of this one person was crucial to the resilience of the organization.

Stay Connected to Stay Resilient

For most of us, resilience comes easiest when we are connected to others. That's why the V tried to isolate us, and that's why we took great risks to keep the lines of communication open. A word of encouragement can boost crushed spirits, ignite flagging hope, and provide vital energy for bouncing back and continuing to persevere.

Sometimes a shared idea or a new perspective on a problem can help someone see a way out. Just knowing someone is near—that you are not standing alone—can provide the needed inspiration, courage, and energy to persevere, even when everything in you is saying it's too tough to keep going. Every soldier, sailor, airman, and marine knows it's not good to fight alone. The same is true in all other organizations. We must stay connected to be resilient.

Foot Stomper: Authentic leaders know that life is difficult. They expect to get knocked down, and they have the proper attitude and outlook to persevere. You have a choice about how you will respond to difficulties. Confront the brutal realities of your situation, but never give up hope. Develop your plan, connect with your support team, and bounce back.

⑦ Coaching: BOUNCE BACK

Resilience is both natural and learned. Reflect on the questions below to identify ways you and others have dealt with setbacks and how those experiences might help you grow in your ability to bounce back.

1. **Look back.** Based on the examples of resilience from this chapter and from the lives of people you know, what lessons can you learn from their experiences? Recall times when you have taken a hit—physically, mentally, professionally, relationally, or financially—and consider how you made comebacks.

2. **Look at your current situation.** What have you learned about resilience that could help you deal more effectively with troublesome issues you are experiencing now? Who might gain resilience from your mentoring, coaching, or encouragement?

3. **Look ahead.** What mindset or principles about resilience could you adopt that would serve you well in the future?

4. **Connect with others.** What family members, friends, mentors, coaches, or other people around you regularly offer you support and encouragement?

Note: To download an expanded version of these coaching questions for writing your responses, visit LeadingWithHonor.com/Book.

---

[1] From the poem "If" by Rudyard Kipling. Someone had memorized this poem before capture, and it was passed through the cell walls and throughout the camps. Most of us memorized it as part of our quest for knowledge, and we were inspired by it in the process.

[2] The Briarpatch was notorious for terrible conditions, ongoing torture, and near freezing temperatures in winter. Thankfully it closed before I arrived in the system.

[3] The move back to the Hilton was precipitated by the raid at Camp Son Tay on 21 November 1970. A few months before, we had been moved out of Son Tay to a new camp about ten miles away. The V had no idea the raid was coming; they moved us to improve our treatment. Camp Faith, as we called it, was most likely a show place to demonstrate to the media that we were being treated well.

[4] *P.O.W. NETWORK*, http://www.pownetwork.org/bios/s/s116.htm (accessed April 17, 2011).

[5] The Stockdale Paradox was the way we lived every day in the camps. Admiral Stockdale and author Jim Collins *(Good to Great)* did everyone a favor by clarifying the statement and making it more widely known. Here Capt Reynolds is using it in a slightly different way. We were confronting the brutal realities, but some were losing hope –"which you can never afford to do."

[6] Louise Harris was the first Air Force MIA wife, and the Air Force bureaucracy ruled that Smitty's normal pay would be withheld and that she would be given only a pittance allotment. In a phone call with the Secretary of the Air Force (SECAF), Louise told him very directly that that was insufficient for supporting three children and totally unacceptable, and that she expected him to fix it promptly. Within the week the SECAF relented and resumed the allotment of Smitty's full pay. The VA wanted her to get Smitty's signature before approving her loan guarantee for purchasing a home. Of course, that was ridiculous, since he was unreachable in the Hanoi Hilton. When Louise explained the situation to Senator Stennis, he recognized the unreasonableness of this inflexible and insensitive policy. His call to the VA brought a quick change in attitude.

[7] Thousands of citizens from across the country purchased and wore these bracelets with names of POW/MIA servicemen. I still occasionally receive a letter or email from someone who wore a POW/MIA bracelet bearing my name and shoot-down date. The bracelets created a strong bond with our cause and us and resulted in many people praying for us by name daily.

[8] James B. Stockdale and Sybil Stockdale, *In Love and War: Jim and Sybil Stockdale.* (New York, NY: Harper & Row, 1984) 378-380.

[9] *Dictionary.com Unabridged*, s.v. "Resilience," http://dictionary.reference.com/browse/resilience (accessed September 30, 2011).

[10] Donald T. Phillips, *The Founding Fathers on Leadership.* (New York, NY: Warner Business Books, 1997) 181-192.

[11] A high percentage of the POWs had been Scouts growing up, and even those who were not knew the oath. It was a powerful force in the POW camps, reinforcing our military training on the principles of duty, honor, responsibility, and faithfulness.

BOY SCOUT OATH (PROMISE)
On my honor I will do my best
to do my duty to God and my country ....

LEADING
OTHERS

Chapter 7

CLARIFY AND
BUILD YOUR CULTURE

*"I came to see, in my decade at IBM,
that culture isn't just one aspect of the
game—it is the game."*

Lou Gerstner, Chairman, and CEO IBM 1993 - 2002

As the senior ranking officer in the camps in the early years, Lt Col Risner wasted no time in issuing simple and direct guidance: *"I'm in charge, and here's what I want you to do. Be a good American. Live by the Code of Conduct. Resist up to the point of permanent physical or mental damage and then no more. Give as little as possible and then bounce back to resist again. Pray every day. Go home proud."* Risner's policies passed quickly through the camps via covert communications, clarifying our mission, vision, and values for what would turn out to be a long war.

Risner made the military Code of Conduct the cornerstone of POW culture. The Defense Department had adopted this code after the Korean War as a tool to help POWs resist Communist exploitation. Virtually every warrior in the U.S. military had memorized it during training, and Risner made it clear that he expected everyone to follow it to the best of his ability.

Just as important as the guidelines Risner issued was the command presence he exhibited. Capt Jon Reynolds experienced Risner's leadership shortly after he arrived. As he lay alone on a concrete slab in the Heartbreak Hotel cellblock of the Hanoi Hilton, Reynolds heard a tap on the wall, then a whisper. It was Risner; he wanted to know the name and condition of this new arrival. Reynolds shared about his broken arms and broken jaw, and that the V had yanked his arms to torture him further.

Risner offered some words of encouragement and said, "Jon, I'm in charge. I want you to resist them to the point of not having permanent mental or physical damage. If you are a praying man, pray often. One of these days, we'll be out of here." To this day Reynolds gratefully recalls Risner's clear commands and calm demeanor. "I hold Risner up as a key reason for my survival. His guidance was so right and so clear."[1]

Risner's first stint as camp SRO did not last long. The V found a written note that contained his guidance and connected it back to him. Determined to squelch his leadership in the camps, they pulled Risner out of the Zoo camp in Hanoi, returned him to Heartbreak Hotel in the Hanoi Hilton (Hoa Lo), and began extensive torture to break him. Because the process for selecting SRO leaders was clearly established, CDR Jerry Denton, the next ranking officer at the Zoo, immediately stepped into the line of fire.

As part of the dramatic change in treatment in the fall of 1965, the V were now torturing men to extract propaganda statements. Denton reaffirmed Risner's policies and added, *"No writing, no taping, take torture until you're in danger of losing mental faculties, and then give a phony story. Die before giving classified information. If broken, don't despair. Bounce back as soon as you can to the hard line. Remember: unity above self."*

Denton's simple motto of "unity above self" provided a strong cultural bond for all of us, even when we were isolated or shuffled from one camp to another. When Denton's strong leadership became evident to the V, they ushered him off to the torture chamber, followed by solitary confinement. Fortunately, James Bond came to the rescue— James Bond Stockdale, that is. Bouncing back from one of his extended periods of abuse and solitary confinement, he took command from his cell in Little Vegas, Thunderbird cellblock, in the spring of 1967. One of his first tasks was to update the policies previously disseminated by Risner and Denton using the clever acronym **"BACK US"**:

B – Bowing: Resist bowing in public; in front of outsiders make the V use force.
> Bowing is a sign of humility and honor in their culture, so rather than let us salute and act like military men, they forced us to bow

down to them, thus humbling us to their authority. We resisted this constantly, forcing them to use physical force to make us bend our heads.

A – Air: Stay off the air, make no recordings for radio and no tapes.
Stockdale had heard that some POWs were reading the *Vietnam Courier* (Hanoi's English-language propaganda paper) over the camp radio. He was concerned that doing this without taking torture was lowering the barrier too much and would bring more requests for our cooperation.

C – Crimes: Don't admit to any crimes.
Stockdale knew men would be tortured to sign confessions, and he was adamant about not giving the V what they wanted. Words like "crimes" or "criminals" should be avoided.

K – Kiss: Don't kiss the enemy goodbye.
If POWs were released, Stockdale did not want them to be overly generous in their comments on the way out.

US – Unity over Self: Stay united; take care of each other.
Cohesion was essential for resistance and survival.

The big three (Risner, Stockdale, and Denton) established the Code of Conduct as the goal, while recognizing that not even the toughest men had been able to live up to a purely literal interpretation. Over time, a somewhat loose-tight culture evolved. It provided strong, clear guidelines, yet allowed each cell SRO, and even each individual, to exercise some judgment in dealing with various situations.

These goals and expectations empowered a common cultural mindset that allowed us to operate with unity across a half dozen camps over a period of several years, whether we were in solitary confinement or locked in large cells. When there was disagreement about local interpretation, we had discussions that sometimes turned into passionate arguments before decisions were made. When necessary, SROs changed or adapted policies as a result of lessons learned.

We were generally free to take a tougher line of resistance than prescribed. Some POWs resisted bowing more than others, or displayed more anger and defiance in the day-to-day relationships with the guards and turnkeys. We were always looking for little ways to gain leverage to improve our situation or negate the nefarious schemes of our captors even when it required painful sacrifices.

The day I received my first package from home is a case in point. As the guards spread the already opened, thoroughly searched contents of the prescribed "six-pound package" before me on the table, I stared longingly at the food items, vitamins, warm socks, and pictures of my family. I had been in captivity for two and a half years, so naturally I was tingling with excitement and anticipation. This package from home promised to be better than the best Christmas present I'd ever received. Yet the experience was tainted by the smirk on the camp officer's face as he affected an attitude of kindness and concern, as though he were my favorite uncle.

As I started to pick up my stuff, he told me I must first sign a receipt. I scanned the document hurriedly and noticed the following sentence: "In accordance with the humane and lenient policy of the Democratic Republic of Vietnam [DRV], I have been allowed to receive a package from my family."

I had heard through our covert communications that there would be a receipt of some sort, and that it would probably be okay to sign it. But now I felt trapped in an agonizing ethical dilemma. I coveted that package; it was the first connection with my family in more than two years. However, only a few months earlier we had been through some very harsh treatment during which two of my cellmates had been singled out for torture. The statement on the receipt wasn't true, and I feared it could be used for propaganda. I had to make a choice between my comfort and my conscience.

When I refused to sign the receipt, the officer picked up the package and told the guard to take me to my cell. Many of the men in the camp, including my cellmates—whom I considered to be exceptionally brave and honorable men—signed the receipt. Their actions were within the policies and boundaries of our culture, and I didn't judge them. Besides, I had seen them sacrifice often for the team, and I totally trusted their commitment. My next package arrived six months later with goodies similar to the first one. But this time there was a special, unexpected bonus: the receipt no longer had a statement about "the lenient and humane treatment" of the DRV. How sweet it was!

Our POW mission statement captured the essence of our culture in the three simple and powerful words: *Return with Honor*. This short phrase provided both a vision and a bond that kept us aligned toward one goal. Framed by the Code of Conduct and shaped by wise leaders, our culture guided and protected us through the dark and difficult years, until we could emerge into the light of freedom at the end of the war. It is not surprising that two of the most famous documentaries about the Vietnam POW experience are titled *Honor Bound* and *Return with Honor*.[2] In addition, the titles of five POW autobiographies contain the word *honor*. Clearly, that word meant a lot in our culture.

⑦ LESSON: CLARIFY AND BUILD YOUR CULTURE

It's easy to appreciate how a strong culture was crucial in the POW camps. Unfortunately, many business leaders don't appreciate how important a strong culture is to the success of their organizations. A strong culture offers two major benefits:

1. It provides overarching clarity and alignment for more effective execution.
2. It creates identity and loyalty, both internally and externally.

Culture Clarifies Mission, Vision, Values

Organizational cultures are shaped by the values and beliefs established by leaders and shared by the people and groups in the organization. Positive cultures increase motivation, teamwork, and commitment. With a clear understanding about core values, operating styles, and standards of behavior, people can focus their talents and energies toward common goals. A common mindset also enables people to operate independently, while remaining aligned with the values and policies of senior leaders.

Establishing a culture requires clarity, commitment, and creativity:

- Clarity about vision, mission, core values, and operational policies
- Commitment to the organization's mission and defined values
- Creativity to make the cultural story unique and compelling

Once the culture is defined, it must be communicated fervently and frequently, until it is caught and bought in every corner and on every level of the organization.

Business growth guru Verne Harnish provides the following practical advice about the tactics and benefits of building strong cultures:

> "Having a few rules, repeating yourself a lot, and acting in ways that are consistent with the rules—these are the three keys, whether you're providing your children with a good moral foundation or providing a company with a strong cultural foundation. And the evidence is irrefutable, that a strong culture leads to superior performance, higher employee retention, and a better-aligned organization."[3]

Culture Reinforces Values

In 1967, Truett Cathy opened the first Chick-fil-A fast-food restaurant in a shopping mall. Today the company serves customers from more than 1,500 locations in thirty-eight states. What's the recipe for this success? After listening to the company's founder and its leaders, and based on my experience with the company as a trainer and a patron, I concluded the primary ingredient is culture, a culture that is clearly defined and diligently followed.

The Chick-fil-A culture is set around the central themes of building strong relationships and exceeding customer expectations. All employees are challenged to serve others with respect and honor through "selfless acts" and "good stewardship." An attitude of servant leadership permeates the company from top to bottom.

In a talk at Southern Methodist University, Mr. Cathy told an attentive audience, "The secret to Chick-fil-A's success is found in Matthew 5:41: 'If someone forces you to go one mile, go with him two miles.' The first mile is about fulfilling customer expectations. Consumers expect to get what they pay for. But if you want to grow your business, you have to go the second mile. That involves building a relationship with everyone who surrounds you. It's about having compassion, learning to obey impulses, and doing what's right."

The company promotes this theme using the expression "2M2N," which is shorthand for "Making the 2nd mile 2nd nature." Some of the "second-mile" examples Cathy cited include providing fresh ground pepper in their restaurants and having fresh flowers on the tables. The 2M2N concept is modeled by the company's leaders and managers, who consider it an honor to serve customers and fellow employees.[4]

"Too often leaders get carried away with results and forget about relationships," says Truett's son Dan, who is now the company's president and CEO. "Customer service is important to us because it's important to the customer. Service is in high demand, but it's in short supply. So we see ourselves as filling a demand."[5]

Chick-fil-A recruits employees who share its values and demonstrate leadership ability. A Leadership Scholarship Program has provided approximately $23 million in financial assistance to 22,000 employees, and the company has received considerable recognition for its gener-osity to the communities it serves. "Business isn't just about making money, but about setting examples and teaching people," says Dan. "The company's priority has never been just to serve chicken. It's to serve a higher calling."

Since its founding in 1967, Chick-fil-A has experienced forty-two successive years of sales increases, with revenues now exceeding $3 billion annually. This brings us back to the thesis of this chapter: Great organizations build unique cultures based around a few values that are critically important to their leaders or founders, and contribute to out-standing customer satisfaction. That's a recipe that drives great results.

Culture Provides Identity, Raises Morale, and Increases Loyalty.

Most military organizations necessarily have strong identities. The Marine Corps probably has the strongest, so strong that the expression "Once a Marine always a Marine" really means something. An Internet search revealed more than four million hits for that expres-sion. My old unit, the 366 Tactical Fighter Wing in Vietnam, was called the "Gunfighters," while our peers flying in the 8th Wing at Ubon,

Thailand, were the "Wolfpack." Some of my Navy friends came from units with more colorful names like VF143, nicknamed the "Pukin Dogs." It seems that their tail logo was supposed to be a black leopard, but since it looked more like a "pukin dog," that's what it became and still is. If a unit is proud of a name like that, you know the culture has to be strong!

Tex Schramm, longtime president and general manager of the Dallas Cowboys used his marketing experiences as a TV producer to build a culture that attracted a national following that persists even though they have not won a championship in many years. In fact they are still 23% more popular than the number 2 NFL franchise in the Nielsen Sports Media Exposure Index[6] and their website gets 50% more hits than the team with the second highest number of web visits.

I realized how popular the NASCAR brand had become a few years ago while facilitating a group of PricewaterhouseCoopers consultants, most of whom were only a few years out of college. During a break in the action, two of the young ladies carried on a long, informed discussion about the Bristol Race, which had occurred the previous weekend. I was amazed to see how NASCAR had transcended its provincial beginnings and gained loyal fans in sophisticated business circles. Dave Kansas, writing for the *Wall Street Journal Online*, says "… the culture of NASCAR, perhaps even more than the racing itself, is elemental to its success. God and family values permeate."[7]

Most civilian organizations with strong cultures also have clear identities. Consider the "Fun" culture of Southwest Airlines that inspires highly dedicated employees to put customer service as their highest goal. Regardless of how you see Southwest's culture, it is the only airline that has been profitable for more than thirty straight years.

IBM was built on the strong culture established by its founder, Thomas Watson. I know one executive who left his role as a sales manager with IBM in the 70s for a better offer, but later decided to return. Once out of the company, he realized the tremendous competitive advantage he had when he walked in a prospect's door with the IBM business card. People trusted the company; when they saw the IBM logo, they knew they were going to receive quality products and services. That reputation sprang from the culture that Watson had drummed into the company many decades before.

During the personal computer revolution of 1985-1992, IBM lost much of its vision, cohesion, and prominence. It suffered serious losses for several years, until CEO Lou Gerstner arrived and provided the necessary leadership to rebuild the company's culture and profitability. His quote at the head of this chapter demonstrates the preeminence he placed on cultural change. Later, in describing how he transformed the "silo mentality" that prevented IBM from delivering cross-functional expertise to customers, he said, "We needed to integrate as a team inside the company, so we could integrate for customers on their premises."

Build Your Culture

Almost paradoxically, some of the most dynamic organizations such as 3M and Apple have a culture that promotes divergent thinking to promote change and innovation. Other organizations have traditional cultures, but allow and even encourage disruptive subcultures in order to keep themselves on the cutting edge. For example, in a speech to the Atlanta CEO Netweavers organization recently, Ralph de la Vega, President and CEO, AT&T Mobility and Consumer Markets, described how their company had one business entity focused strictly on entrepreneurship, seeking out new disruptive technologies that could take advantage of AT&T wireless networks.[8] Notice how each of these organizations is being proactive to shape a culture that fits its needs and values.

If cultures are so important, why do so many leaders shy away from the culture-building process? Perhaps some think it's just "fluffy stuff." Others simply may underestimate the value, or they may wish to escape the accountability a well-defined culture would establish. Regardless, those who resist culture-building are missing the boat.

You'll achieve greatest success as a leader when you use your vision and passion to create an environment that attracts and retains people who have the ability and the desire to help you reach your goals. A strong culture facilitates concerted, productive actions. Building such a culture is foundational to authentic leadership.

Foot Stomper: Authentic leaders intentionally define and build cultures that further the mission, vision, and values of their organization. Assess the culture of your organization and take the appropriate steps to make sure it is well defined, soundly structured, and effectively communicated.

⑦ Coaching: CLARIFY AND BUILD YOUR CULTURE

The most successful leaders promote their culture by communicating its key themes constantly and consistently through a wide variety of channels. They support the culture by establishing hiring, training, and other policies and procedures aligned with it. Have you been intentional about clarifying and building your culture? Answer these questions to see where you stand.

1. **Do you have an authentic culture?** Your culture must be aligned with who you are and who you are committed to becoming. Your walk must match your talk. Describe the key attributes of your organization's culture as it is now. How would you like it to be?

2. **Does your team have clarity about your culture as it relates to mission, vision, and values?** How can you determine this? How can you consistently reinforce the culture with your team and current employees?

3. **How do you hire and indoctrinate new people into your culture?** Do your hiring processes consider culture? If not, how could you improve them?

Note: To download an expanded version of these coaching questions for writing your responses, visit LeadingWithHonor.com/Book.

---

[1] Brig Gen Jon Reynolds, interview by Lee Ellis, "POW Leadership," September 16, 2007.

[2] Stuart I. Rochester and Frederick Kiley, *Honor Bound: American Prisoners of War in Southeast Asia 1961-1973*. (Annapolis, MD: Naval Institute Press, 1999).

"Return with Honor," PBS DVD Video, A Sanders and Mock/American Film Foundation Production, (Burbank, CA: PBS, 2000).

[3] Verne Harnish, *Mastering the Rockefeller Habits*. (New York, NY: SelectBooks, Inc., 2002) 43.

[4] The Daily Campus, http://www.smudailycampus.com/mobile/news/chick-fil-a-shares-stories-of-company-culture-1.1542230 (accessed March 10, 2011).

[5] Michael Hyatt Intentional Leadership, http://michaelhyatt.com/an-interview-with-dan-cathy.html (accessed April 13, 2011).

[6] Nielsen Sports Media Exposure Index, a new rating system that made its debut in September 2009, uses several criteria to determine each NFL team's popularity.

[7] Dave Kansas, "Editorial Page," *Wall Street Journal Online*, http://online.wsj.com/article/0,,SB106194970566142100.html (accessed November 16, 2010).

[8] Ralph de la Vega moved on to become Vice Chairman and retired in January 2017.

Chapter 8

OVER-COMMUNICATE
THE MESSAGE

★

"Without communications, no one would have survived.
It was the bedrock of everything we did,
and the glue that kept us together as a unit."

Rear Admiral R. Byron Fuller, US Navy (Ret).
Vietnam POW 1967-1973

The bleakest aspect of our existence that first winter was our sense of isolation. The four of us confined in that gloomy, maximum security cell were shut off from the world. We didn't know the identity of the other American POWs in the compound, and they didn't know about us. Isolation heightened our fears, especially when the V began daily programs on the camp radio about war crimes, indicating that those who did not repent would be dealt with harshly. If bad things happened to us, no one would ever know. Thankfully, the arrival of warmer spring weather revived our spirits and renewed our hope and energy to fight this psychological battle.

One afternoon we heard an American voice whispering through our window from the interior courtyard: "Can you hear me in there?" I scampered onto the upper bunk nearest the window and pressed my head against the bars of the 16" x 24" opening. To increase our sense of isolation and keep us from observing other POWs, the V had covered the opening with a rattan mat, but a four-inch gap between the outside wall of our cell and the mat gave me just enough space to look down and see a grinning face.

"Hi. My name is Bill Tschudy {LTJG, USN}. Do you know the code?" When I replied in the negative, he said, "It's a five by five matrix. A is 1-1; B is 1-2." Suddenly guards appeared and slapped Tschudy away from our window. It happened so fast that I could not fully grasp the matrix concept, but when I relayed the basics to my cellmates, Jim Warner recognized it as the same code he had read about in Arthur Koestler's book *Darkness at Noon*. In this novel, the prisoner hero used this five by five code to combat communist exploitation in the Soviet gulag. Now thirty years later, American POWs were using it to resist communist exploitation in the POW camps of North Vietnam.

Based on what Tschudy (LT USN) had said and on Jim's incredible memory, we figured out that the five by five matrix contained twenty-five letters of the alphabet. But since the alphabet contains twenty-six letters, we didn't have quite enough information to make the matrix work consistently.

During siesta time one day, Sweet Pea hurriedly shoved another POW into our cell. What a surprise to suddenly be face-to-face with another American! It was Air Force Captain Dave Ford, and after exchanging some basic facts about our backgrounds, he gave us the missing piece of the puzzle: the letter "C" was also used for the letter "K".[1]

At chow time later that afternoon, when Sweet Pea opened the door and saw five of us instead of four, his eyes popped. He grabbed Dave and dragged him to his proper cell across the hall; we didn't see Dave again for several years. Sweet Pea, who apparently had mistaken Dave for me, must have confessed his errors at the party meeting that night, because he was missing two stripes the next day and thereafter was noticeably contrite around us.

But Sweet Pea's loss was our gain, for now we knew the missing letter and could use the code. The first tap was for the row, and the second tap was for the column. For example, the word "Hi" would be composed of *down 2 and over 3* for the letter "H," and *down 2 and over 4* for the letter "i." Thus, tapping "Hi" would sound like this: *tap tap* pause; *tap tap tap* pause; *tap tap* pause; *tap tap tap tap*.

Across Second

	1	2	3	4	5
1	A	B	C	D	E
2	F	G	**H**	**I**	J
3	L	M	N	O	P
4	Q	R	S	T	U
5	V	W	X	Y	Z

Down First

H is down 2 and over 3 (tapped 2 – 3)
I is down 2 and over 4 (tapped 2 – 4)

It would be difficult to overemphasize how much that code lifted our spirits. I felt like a starving man who had just been given filet mignon with all the trimmings. Never again would I take communications for granted. Over time, because of the code, we were able to find out who was in the camp, connect into the chain of command, and function as a team. We could now keep each other abreast of the enemy's tactics and the best countermeasures to undermine them. And it was extraordinarily reassuring to know that Americans outside our cell knew that we were alive.

Learning the code became an obsession for me. I practiced by lightly tapping out virtually every thought that came into my mind. Soon I could communicate without consciously thinking about the code, in the same way that a proficient typist doesn't need to look at the keyboard, or someone fluent in a language doesn't think about the individual words. Miss McDougal, my tenth-grade typing teacher, would have been astounded that I could accomplish such speed and accuracy with my fingers.

Once the rhythm and beat of the tap code became imbedded in our heads, we noticed that many sounds in the compound were actually code. Often we would hear guys at the clothesline shake and snap their washing to send a quick message. Since our cell had no common walls that we could use for tapping, I adopted the bamboo-stick washroom broom as my communications instrument of choice. As I swished the green scum on the wet brick floor, my messages echoed out of the roofless washroom and across the courtyard, as if projected from a megaphone.

We usually repeated important messages to make sure they were received. One cell would send out the message in the morning, and another would use a different method to transmit the same message after lunch. Redundancy was essential because, as in the "real world," many people didn't get the word the first time.

It took considerable time to transmit a message, but time was one resource we had in abundance. Any productive activity that also killed time was a blessing. To speed transmission, we invented a shorthand, similar to what is now commonplace with text messaging. For example,

wn was *when*,
tt was *that*,
CUL (see you later) was *goodbye*,
and *GBU* (God bless you) was the typical signoff at the end of the day.

At times the prison walls sounded as if they were being attacked by a horde of hungry woodpeckers. We became so proficient at communicating in code that we joked about how some of the more reserved guys, when they were released and got home, would prefer tapping to talking.

The conditions at Son Tay camp provided better visibility of guard activity, which allowed us to safely transmit tap-code messages from one building to another using flashes or flags. We also learned that if we rolled a blanket into a horse collar or doughnut shape to serve as a muffler, we could literally shout through sixteen-inch concrete-block walls and not be heard outside.

Clearing was hard work.
Drawing by former POW Mike McGrath[2]

Using a blanket muffler,
I could talk through a 16" wall.
Drawing by former POW Mike McGrath[2]

Communications was a major team effort. The "clearers" who kept a lookout for guards had the hardest job; they often had to remain in cramped positions for hours. By necessity, we all became skilled actors. When guards snapped open the peephole in our cell door to check on us, they would see only lethargic POWs with the most innocent poses and expressions imaginable. It was like a child's game of cat and mouse, but with very high stakes.

As one of the primary communicators between our building (Cat House) and the other two across the compound (Beer Hall and Opium Den), I was plenty busy. We sent and received everything from daily situation reports on health and camp operations, to the enemy's latest schemes for coercion. When business-message traffic was slow, we sent personal news and stories that would be of interest to all. Later, we sped up communications by using the hand code. The physical conditions of the cells dictated the communication methods.

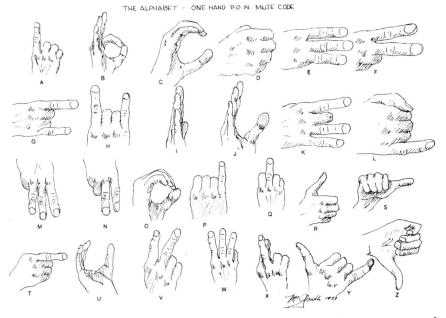

Hand (mute) code expedited communications. Drawing by former POW Mike McGrath[3]

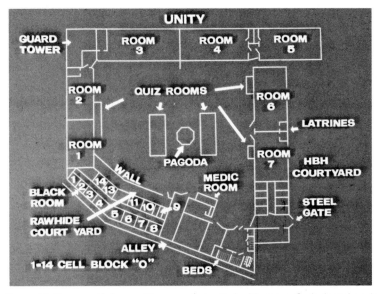

Camp Unity room 3 (my cell) communicated with room 2 via hand code. Adjacent rooms could not see each other and communicated using the blanket to talk through the walls.

In the latter years of our captivity, when more of us were together in larger rooms, we instituted two channels for passing messages from room to room. One was for regular types of communication, and the other channel was for "classified" information, such as escape plans and discipline problems. Only a few men would be allowed to handle this classified information and then only on a need-to-know basis.

It would be safe to say that in the early years and small cells, 50 percent of our waking hours were spent in covert communications. Later, in the larger cells, fewer people were needed, and with our newer technologies and a less threatening environment, communications were much more efficient. Over the years we used tap code, hand code, flash code, Morse code, cough/hack/spit code, sweeping code, voices through walls, notes over walls, notes under doors, and more. Because they knew it was our primary tool for resistance, the V tried hard to stop us, but they never could.

In the summer of 1969, when American families back home were celebrating the lunar landing, American POWs were suffering badly. An escape attempt at the Zoo had the V looking for any excuse to whip us into line. Fearful we had an escape plan, the V began torturing our SRO Capt Ken Fisher. We had none, but Ken was strapped to a stool in leg irons and kept awake for twenty-one days. Though delirious, he gave them nothing and resisted until they returned him to our cell. Captains Jay Jayroe and Wes Schierman (USAF) and Captain Orson Swindle (USMC) refused to sign "good treatment" propaganda statements, so they got similar torture. After more than two weeks without sleep, the guards began beating them. Eventually they signed a "no value" statement, giving the V a way to save face.[4]

Meanwhile, because of poor treatment, Smitty Harris and Fred Flom (1st Lt, USAF) were fighting losing battles with a debilitating gastrointestinal disease. Through a crack in our door we watched Smitty and Fred stagger across the courtyard to the bathhouse, their emaciated bodies reminiscent of survivors of Auschwitz and Bataan. Smitty's POW weight had dwindled from 130 pounds to about ninety. Fred's had dropped from about 140 down to about 110.

Son Tay SRO Lieutenant Commander Render Crayton realized it would take drastic action to save the lives of these men. Using the tap code, he sent an urgent message that was transmitted across the entire compound: "Tell every English-speaking Vietnamese you meet that the camp commander must do something for Harris and Flom, or his superiors in Hanoi are going to be very upset with him about what is going to happen in this camp.'"

By threatening to make trouble, we were virtually inviting reprisal. This ploy was especially risky because it revealed that we had a cohesive team with good communications. Once the enemy realized that we were organized as a military unit with a functioning operational leader, they might try to break us. Nevertheless, the seriousness of the situation justified the risk.

The next day, POWs across the camp delivered the bold, agreed-upon message in rapid-fire succession. If only one or two guards had received the message, the V would have downplayed it. But our "over-communication" resounded across the camp like a string of firecrackers that couldn't be ignored.

Evidently, the V camp commander, fearful for his job, was convinced we had the will and capability to carry out our threat. Three days after the message hit, Smitty and Fred were taken to a field hospital a few miles away and given a fluoroscope. This was followed by two shots twice daily that were apparently vitamins and antibiotics. Their improvement was slow but steady. A year later, they were back up to their normal POW weight.

It's superbly fitting that the code was instrumental in saving Smitty Harris's life, because Smitty was the man who saved all of us by bringing the tap code to the POW camps. In fact, he was known to us as the "code bearer." When Smitty was in survival school, he alone stayed after class one day to learn about the code used by POWs in World War II. Then as one of the first POWs in the war, he passed on this precious gift to his fellow prisoners. Now, four years later, the code had come full circle and saved his life.

⑦ LESSON: OVER-COMMUNICATE THE MESSAGE

In the POW camps, communication was our primary weapon in the daily battle against an aggressive and determined enemy who constantly sought to isolate us. Their goal was to prevent us from working as a cohesive team, so they could pick us off one by one. Communication was so crucial for survival, in fact, that it became second nature for us to "over-communicate." We learned that successful communication requires *redundancy* and *multiplicity* to connect with various learning styles. To ensure that an important message was received and understood, we always sent it numerous times through multiple channels.

In the workplace, the adversaries of good communications are not so obvious as in the POW camps, but they're just as powerful. The "noise" created by the busyness, distractions, and competing agendas of every organization can shut out communications just as effectively as the most depraved flesh-and-blood enemy.

Most of us understand how poor communication can disrupt unity, but we often fail to appreciate how much it can undermine successful execution. Reflect for a moment on this list of typical problems that occur when leaders fail to intentionally and diligently over-communicate:

1. Uncoordinated actions cause
   - Duplication of effort.
   - Failure to share best practices.
   - Friction and unnecessary competition.
   - Wasted energy.
2. Projects don't get completed on schedule due to inaction and slippage.
3. Wrong actions result in costly mistakes.
4. Bad assumptions lead to bad decisions and bad outcomes.
5. Decision-making becomes disconnected from values,

strategies, and policies.

6. Departmental silos undermine needed cross-functional communication.

7. Frustration and fears begin to erode morale and energy.

8. People move into a survival mode and
   • Cohesion breaks down.
   • Teamwork degenerates to every person "looking out for number one."

9. Mission effectiveness degrades and morale plummets.

10. High performers begin looking for a way out.

Unfortunately, very few leaders appreciate the importance of over-communicating. They assume that communicating something once or twice is sufficient, but nothing could be further from the truth. When their message is received, it's often not understood with sufficient clarity to produce the desired results.

An Air Force study examining leadership challenges found that poor communication was the most significant obstacle to effective leadership.[5] Effective leaders come to understand that they must over-communicate in order to actually get through. They hone their message on a particular issue until it is crystal clear, and then they put it out over and over in personal conversations, speeches, presentations, memos, press releases, white papers, phone calls, newsletters, posters, graphics, and more. When they start to feel like a "broken record"—thoroughly bored listening to themselves communicate the same message time and again—they know they're just beginning to communicate effectively.

In his national best selling book *The Four Obsessions of an Extraordinary Executive*, Patrick Lencioni highlights the four disciplines of great leaders. He says the third discipline, over-communicate, is the "simplest," but it's also the one "most underachieved." To effectively communicate, says Lencioni, a *simple* message must be *repeatedly* delivered in a *cascading* manner through *multiple* channels.[6]

That's exactly what Marie Mouchet did when she took over as VP and CIO for two (and later three) key divisions of Southern Company, a Fortune 200 electric utility company. Marie already had established a track record as a strong leader, but success in her new role was far from certain. The IT departments were struggling to keep pace with the rapid advances in information technology; customer response was slow. She faced a serious and difficult situation.

Marie started with an offsite teambuilding retreat, where she and her management team discussed Lencioni's four disciplines and how they could be applied. While they were building cohesion (Lencioni's first discipline), they practiced the second discipline by clarifying their vision and developing strategies for realizing it. Then they began implementing Lencioni's third discipline by communicating this message over and over at every opportunity, until all levels of the organization internalized it. Managers enthusiastically bought in to the campaign, because they helped develop the message. Over the next two years, Marie executed Lencioni's fourth discipline by hiring, building, and managing human systems that supported their goals, their values, and their commitment to transparency and clear communications.

In weekly huddles, one-on-one meetings, and coaching sessions, the management team refined its strategies and fine-tuned its message. Online updates kept all team members apprised of the progress of projects, shared concerns, and breakthroughs. Quarterly webcasts and semiannual employee meetings allowed everyone to get to know Marie, at least virtually. She used these forums to explain, endorse, emphasize, and reiterate the organization's vision, mission, and goals. The central focus was understanding and serving the company's business units and senior leaders.

A believer in 360 degree communications, Marie and her managers used individual and group meetings to get to know their clients and understand their needs. Each year customers were invited to turn in scorecards on IT's performance. Marie and her team used this feedback to correct deficiencies, so that customer satisfaction consistently improved. The turnaround has been a great success. Cohesive teamwork, clarity about mission and strategies, and over-communication internally and with customers across three divisions of a sprawling company have enabled IT to become highly regarded as a valuable member of the business team.

Marie Mouchet has distinguished herself as an outstanding manager and communicator. In 2007 she was recognized by the Women in Technology organization as Woman of the Year for Enterprise, and in 2009 Computerworld Magazine named her one of the nation's Premier 100 IT Leaders.

We all have many things vying for our attention. Unless we hear something several times and in several places, we don't take it seriously. Media experts know that a message must be repeated several times before people pay attention. After people hear the same message several times, they start to get it; they begin to realize that you mean what you say.

Good communication alone won't guarantee positive results, but poor communication almost always guarantees disappointing performance.

Foot Stomper: Effective communication requires intentional effort. To overcome the noise, distractions, and misinterpretations in the workplace, you must develop a clear message and a comprehensive communication plan. Then you must over-communicate your message multiple times through multiple channels.

⑦ Coaching: OVER-COMMUNICATE THE MESSAGE

The leader is the quarterback and head communicator on the team. Clear signal calling is essential in order for others to execute their responsibilities. Regardless of how well your organization is performing, an objective look at your communication effectiveness will usually reveal that more emphasis and effort will pay significant dividends.

1. **How do your natural traits affect your communications?** After reflection, answer "a" or "b" below as appropriate. Then ask for honest feedback.

   a. If your natural personality is more **introverted**
      - You probably have a tendency to under-communicate. Could this be a problem? If so, you'll have to get out of your comfort zone to improve.
      - You may assume others know what you know and think what you think. Do these assumptions cause problems for your team?

   b. If your natural personality is more **extroverted**
      - You may talk a lot without communicating a clear and focused message. Could this be a problem? How could you communicate more effectively?
      - Do your people know that you tend to "talk to think" and therefore may express opinions on issues before you have analyzed or committed to them? Would calling this to their attention be helpful?

2. **What changes would you like to make in your communications?** Would it help to be intentional about over-communicating your messages? Are you communicating a consistent message, repeated in multiple settings? Are you using a variety of media and channels to get the word out?

Note: To download an expanded version of these coaching questions for writing your responses, visit LeadingWithHonor.com/Book.

[1] Some cells tapped 2-6 for "K" instead of using C for "K."

[2] John M. McGrath, *Prisoner of War: Six Years in Hanoi.* (Annapolis, MD: Naval Institute Press, 1975) 33, 37.

[3] McGrath, 41.

[4] This was typical of the way in which our communist captors unapologetically used the most evil means to achieve their goals. Lesson: beware of leaders who use their end goals to justify their questionable or unethical means.

[5] Based on a survey of more than 500 USAF members. Richard I. Lester, PhD. "Top Ten Management Concerns." Paul Hersey, Kenneth Blanchard and Dewey Johnson, *Management of Organizational Behavior*, 7th ed. (Upper Saddle River, NJ: Prentice Hall, 1996) 8.

[6] Patrick Lencioni, *The Four Obsessions of an Extraordinary Executive.* (San Francisco, CA: Jossey-Bass, A Wiley Company, 2000) 167.

Chapter 9

DEVELOP YOUR PEOPLE

★

"Any organization develops people:
it has no choice. It either helps
them grow or stunts them."

Peter Drucker

Military professionals by nature are action-oriented high achievers who want to make the most of every opportunity. Even though our futures were uncertain and our resources were sparse, we looked for activities that would give us some measure of growth and accomplishment. We were motivated simply by the desire to sharpen our minds and develop knowledge and skills that someday might be helpful.

When the mind is free from clutter, it's amazing how memory and cognitive effectiveness improve.[1] After our release, the intelligence officers who debriefed us were astonished at the level of detail we could recall. Most of us could remember the exact dates—even the days of the week—of every significant event in our lives as POWs.

As we moved around from camp to camp and engaged in covert communications, most of us collected the names of the POWs in the Hanoi system. At one point, I had memorized in alphabetical order more than a hundred and fifty names. But cellmate Navy LCDR JB McKamey won the prize. Almost daily he paced around the cell reciting the names of nearly three hundred POWs.

Before my deployment to Southeast Asia, Air Force 1st Lt Lance Sijan and I had been dormmates and golfing buddies. At Son Tay camp, I learned that his plane had gone down one day after mine. Badly injured, he survived in the jungles of Laos for forty-six days before being captured. His remarkable story was not a surprise. Throughout our training he was always keen about his professional development. Lance stood out in survival school because he appeared to be the most highly motivated learner, both in the classroom and on the mountain trek.

As Ron Mastin (1st Lt, USAF) flashed Lance's painful story across the camp to our building, I put the pieces together. I remembered our first winter of captivity, when my cellmates and I had listened helplessly as someone in a cell down the hall deliriously cried out for help. I summoned the officer in charge, and a few minutes later Fat in the Fire opened the peephole in our door. "Please, will you help this man?" I pleaded. With a serious look on his face he replied, "He has bad head injury. Been in jungle too long. Has one foot in grave." He slammed the peephole shut and left.

Of course, in the isolated cells of Thunderbird, we had no way of knowing who was dying. Two years later, I realized that we had been audible witnesses to Lance's last valiant struggle to survive.[2] After the war, we learned more details of Lance's heroic actions to evade, escape, and endure. His courageous efforts to resist, survive, escape, and return with honor were so notable that he was awarded the Congressional Medal of Honor (posthumously). One of the Air Force's most prestigious annual awards for leadership is named the Sijan Award.

We POWs spent many hours remembering incidents and people from our past. When I couldn't recall someone's name, I would concentrate until it came to me. Sometimes it would take a couple of weeks, but eventually the name would pop into my mind or come to me in a dream. Once I spent several days recalling the names of everybody in my eighth grade class. I could remember where they sat, what the classroom looked like, and what we studied.

When I came home, people in my home town of Commerce, Georgia, were amazed at how well I remembered their names. Of course, I had met very few new people over those five-plus years as a POW, and I had kept old acquaintances and friends alive in my mind through daily reflections and mental exercise.

During my second year of incarceration, I began to put my imagination to work on specific projects. For example, I mentally operated a forty-acre farm. I designed and built the fences; purchased livestock and the farm equipment; calculated the costs for planting, fertilizing, cultivating, and harvesting the crops; set the selling prices; and calculated the profits. Naturally, I exempted myself from taxes.

I would spend as many as ten hours a day on this project, sometimes working my brain so hard that I got an intense headache. At the end of four weeks—which I had mentally expanded into several growing seasons—I owned most of the land in the county, as well as my own feed mills and a railroad siding for shipping. Running an imaginary farm business sharpened my math and reasoning skills and made it easier for me to catch up with my peers academically when I returned home. The experience also proved useful when I bought and operated a sixty-four-acre Texas grain sorghum farm near San Antonio five years after my release.

The next project was stimulated by my interest in becoming an attorney. I spent several weeks deciding what kind of lawyer I would be and where I would go to school. After quite a lot of research using our covert communication system, I decided that I would attend the University of Virginia law school and become a tax attorney. Most of the POWs engaged in similar "Walter Mitty" fantasies, which sound somewhat bizarre now, but in that environment helped preserve our sanity.

Although I've never had much time for golf, I enjoy the game. So I exercised my mind during my 1,955 days of captivity by remembering most of the courses I had played. Sometimes it would take me several days, but I could eventually remember all eighteen holes on a golf course I had played only three or four times. I would replay each hole, remembering where the sand traps and other features were and what shots I had actually made. I also could remember many of the shots my former golfing buddy Lance Sijan had made. In my memory, as in real life, he drove the ball much farther than I.

One day the turnkey inadvertently left the shutters open on a nearby cell, and I saw a fellow POW (future cellmate Air Force Captain Bob Peel) practicing his typing on an imaginary typewriter. That seemed like a brilliant idea, so I started doing the same. When I returned home, I could type faster and more accurately than ever. What a blessing that turned out to be in this age of computers.

Our captors surprised us with a rudimentary chess set one day, which they had allowed the POWs in another cell to make. The board was made from cardboard, and the pieces were flat strips of brown toilet paper layered and glued together, with the first letter of each piece neatly labeled. Ken, Jim, and I spent so much time playing that we learned to see the chessboard in our minds. At bedtime, we would lie on the hard boards that were our bunks and mentally review every move of that day's game.

By temperament I am an action person, and in my pre-Vietnam days I didn't generally like to take time for board games and complex thinking. But playing chess and bridge developed my ability to focus deeply and think logically. By the time I returned home, my mind had a remarkable facility for memorization, visualization, and conceptualization, and I could do rather complex math problems in my head. Although this mental agility has diminished with time due to the "noise" and information overload of modern life, a fair amount is still with me and has proved to be extremely beneficial. Without it, I doubt that I could have written this book.

Unity compound of Hoa Loa (Hanoi Hilton): Note dish rack and water tank for bath and washing in courtyard.

Even though Camp Unity had much larger rooms—my cell measured about twenty-five feet by seventy feet—fifty-five of us were jammed in there like sardines, twenty-four hours a day, seven days a week. Fortunately there was adequate space to walk.

We never knew if or when there might be another rescue attempt, and Lt Col Risner, now our camp director of operations, wanted to make sure we were physically able to walk out of captivity if the opportunity arose. He asked all room SROs to test each man's fitness and send back a report. Our room SRO, Lieutenant Commander Doug Clower, suspended all other activities for a day and took us on a ten-mile hike around the perimeter of our cell. If the guards peeked in, they probably wondered why fifty-five men were pacing all day around this small room. The hardest part for me was just keeping up with my long-legged friend and mentor Capt Jay Jayroe. This different activity was fun, and it boosted our morale when everyone made it.

In such close quarters, SRO Clower quickly realized that things could get dicey if we didn't have activities to occupy our time. So he asked Captain Tom Storey (USAF), an experienced educator, to launch a learning program. Tom listed various study options using the concrete slab floor as his blackboard and pieces of broken brick as chalk. The electives included math, calculus, science, history, Spanish, German, French, electronics, German wines, and public speaking.

That evening around sundown, we had our regular room meeting to make announcements, celebrate birthdays, acknowledge shoot-down anniversaries, and engage in a brief period of silence, which was our transition from the daytime to the evening schedule. With fifty-five of us constantly chatting and moving, it was our only time all day for quiet reflection and meditation. During announcements, Tom shared his plans and invited us to use the "chalk" to mark our course preferences. Based on this survey, he organized the subjects and recruited the most qualified instructors.

One track of courses was taught on Monday, Wednesday, and Friday, and another on Tuesday, Thursday, and Saturday. School was in session three hours in the mornings and two hours in the afternoons.

On selected nights during the week we would have special interest programs, when someone might talk about a book he had read, a movie he had seen, or a trip he had taken. A Toastmasters public speaking group met at one end of the room two nights a week. On Sunday mornings we had a church service, complete with a choir of eight guys who actually could sing.

I taught basic French and studied basic Spanish and German, as well as intermediate French. For about a year, two other guys and I practiced these three languages fifteen minutes a day, six days a week. My goal was to become fluent in French and Spanish and have a two-thousand-word working vocabulary in German. The good news is that I achieved my goals. The bad news is that I was a POW long enough to accomplish these goals and many others.

We had no books, so all subjects were taught from memory. It's remarkable how much talent resided in that group of military men. For example, Navy LT Denver Key, with whom I shared a cell for almost four years, taught a small group of us differential calculus. We wrote our problems on the concrete-slab floor using pieces of brick as chalk. Denver loved math and had a gift for teaching, so the class was fun and we learned a lot.

In the camps we had alumni from elite schools like MIT, Stanford, Notre Dame, Georgia Tech, Purdue, Duke, and all three service academies. But in fields other than math and engineering, Jim Warner was like a one-man university, He had an unquenchable curiosity, a photographic mind, and a remarkable memory. He was literally a "walking encyclopedia."

In fact, that's where it all started. When Warner was six or seven, his parents bought an encyclopedia set from a door-to-door salesman. Jim read it from A-Z and still remembered much of it. He loved literature, history, politics, and science, and could recall the most notable ideas of every major philosopher in Western culture. He spoke French, Spanish, and some German, and he could read Latin. Fortunately for our self-esteem, there were a few things he didn't know. For instance, he wasn't aware that one could buy a car for less than the sticker price.

Memorizing poetry was a popular project throughout the camps. People who had memorized various works contributed them to our "library," so they could be used by others. Typical poems that most of us memorized included "The Highwayman" by Alfred Noyse, "Ballad of East and West" and "If" by Rudyard Kipling, "The Cremation of Sam McGee" by Robert Service, and "The Gift Outright," which Robert Frost delivered at President Kennedy's inauguration. Many of the men also memorized scripture, especially Psalms 1, 23, and 100.

Most cells had similar ongoing educational programs, and someone came up with the idea of organizing an officer candidate school for the only three Air Force enlisted men in the Hanoi POW camps. A number of officers developed a rigorous curriculum and volunteered to teach the various components of the course. When the three men returned home, the United States Congress approved the program and offered the candidates commissions as second lieutenants in the U.S. Air Force. One was close to retirement, so he declined. The other two men accepted their commissions and enjoyed successful careers.

The lack of books or outside resources did not limit our continuous learning in the POW camps. We relied on recall of past education, and where there was a lack of clarity on a subject, we tried to get a consensus of the best minds. Eventually many areas were codified into what we called "Hanoi Fact"— meaning it was accepted as true until we were released and could verify the information. The in-house joke was that some men whose education had been slighted before capture and now proudly posed as experts, had been totally educated by Hanoi Fact. Fortunately, it turned out that our facts were amazingly accurate. Our investment in development has paid big dividends in the years since.

⑦ LESSON: DEVELOP YOUR PEOPLE

American military training is unsurpassed. It has to be, because combat is literally a matter of life and death. Training in the armed services is an ongoing process, not simply a series of one-time events. For example, ground egress and ejection seat training were required every six months in peacetime, and at least monthly when we were in combat. I was certainly thankful for that when I had to eject over enemy territory. In fact, I'm amazed and very grateful for how the on-going preparation I received enabled me so many times in my career to make decisions and take actions calmly and efficiently in the midst of crises.

In civilian life, as in the military, preparation and continuous learning supported by consistent reinforcement are crucial for sustained success. Not surprisingly, research shows that the companies who invest in high-quality, on-going training are more profitable than those who don't.[3] Building "muscle memory" and confidence is vital for reliable execution, especially under pressure. Training-and-development pros know that isolated training events seldom develop genuine competence.

Practice to Become the Best In Your Profession

On January 15, 2009, shortly after takeoff from New York's LaGuardia Airport, US Airways Flight 1549 collided with a flock of birds, causing both engines to flame out. With absolutely no power, Captain Chesley "Sully" Sullenberger's only option was to attempt one of the most difficult feats in aviation: a crash landing on water. He knew if he didn't contact the Hudson River at precisely the right angle, his plane would either break apart or plunge beneath the water's surface. One or two degrees difference in the glide path could mean the difference between life and death for all 155 passengers and crew on board.

Fortunately, there could not have been a better-prepared person flying that aircraft. Sully's entire life since earning a pilot's license at age sixteen had been focused on aviation. At the Air Force Academy, he had graduated as "top flier" and winner of the Outstanding Aviation Award, and he subsequently had distinguished himself as a top fighter pilot in the Air Force.

When Sully left military service to become a commercial pilot, he maintained his commitment to continuous learning and improvement. He was so knowledgeable, in fact, that he was often called as an expert witness during aviation inquiries. On that fateful day over New York City, Captain Sullenberger drew on forty years of aviation experience that included 27,000 hours of flight time, hundreds of hours of flight simulator training, years of regular classroom instruction, and an extensive background of technical research into flying safety.

Anyone who has seen the video of Sully's landing can't help but marvel at his precise execution. Many military and commercial pilots have lost an engine to birds somewhere along the way, but few have ever lost all their engines and lived to tell about it. It's even more astounding that Sully and his crew accomplished this feat in a large commercial airliner over a major city without a single loss of life. This "miracle on the Hudson," which earned Sully the number two spot on *Time* magazine's list of the Top 100 Most Influential Heroes and Icons of 2009, resoundingly testifies to the value of thorough preparation and continuous learning.

In his best-selling book, *The Talent Code: Greatness Isn't Born. It's Grown. Here's How.*, Daniel Coyle says that it takes about ten thousand hours of "deep practice" for professionals to become tops in their field. The author points out that top athletes, great musicians, and other performers all have coaches, and they practice much more than they perform. For example, the top professional golfers typically hit three hundred to four hundred balls a day.

Likewise, outstanding organizational leaders are always learning and growing. They practice their skills, benefit from coaching, gain awareness of their performance through regular critiques, and hone their abilities through continuous development. On the other hand, less successful leaders typically spend so much time "performing" that they have no time for "practice," and the thought of having a professional coach is foreign to them.

Follow the Continuous Development Model

The diagram below depicts the development method used by virtually all highly successful individuals and organizations. When I employ this process with my executive coaching clients, they're able to achieve increasingly higher levels of performance with each cycle.

KNOWLEDGE ⟶ PLAN ⟶ EXECUTE

REPEAT THE PROCESS ⟵ ANALYZE AND CRITIQUE

Continuous Development Model

A few years ago I collaborated in a team-building exercise with Ron Mumm, who at that time was the director of flight operations and chief pilot for BellSouth Aviation. As a Lieutenant Colonel in the Air Force, he had commanded the Thunderbirds demonstration team, a hand-picked group of the finest fighter pilots in the world. Ron credited his team's outstanding performance to this continuous preparation-and-critique development concept. The Thunderbirds debriefed after every practice session and after every show by analyzing each maneuver. They integrated their ideas into a plan and put their plan into action the following day. Then they repeated the entire process. Ron often said, "Those who are passionate about performance must be passionate about critique and practice."

Whether it's the Thunderbirds, Blue Angels, Navy SEALs, Southwest Airlines, IBM, American Idol, or leadership development with a coach, this continuous development process is the proven way to raise performance levels. Talent is important, but talent without continuous development will quickly peak. To grow your skills so you can lead higher, you must first gain awareness. With knowledge you can plan, execute, and critique key components of every important action.

Learn from the Success of a Large Healthcare System

Since 2003, I have conducted ongoing leadership development processes with the senior team of Northeast Georgia Health System (NGHS) in Gainesville, Georgia. Carol Burrell, EVP and COO (now CEO), and Tracy Vardeman, VP Strategic Planning and Marketing, were the prime movers who kept this process going over a number of years. Our initial sessions focused on trust building, creative conflict, and emotional intelligence. Based on this information and on feedback from behavioral assessments, 360 assessments, and peer reviews, all participants created written development plans, shared their goals with peers, and participated in ongoing coaching. Along the way, they put into practice what they had learned, while regularly giving each other feedback on progress made and opportunities missed.

As the organization's coach, I admired the strength and motivation of the leadership team. Their emotional maturity allowed them to be receptive to peer feedback and coaching, which in turn accelerated their personal and professional growth. Their teamwork and leadership seemed to be quite strong, but I was not sure how well they were performing compared to national standards.

Then, in 2010, the report card came in. Thompson-Reuters recognized NGHS as one of the nation's "100 Top Hospitals." What's more, NGHS was one of only 23 in the 100 Top Hospitals to receive the Everest Award, which recognizes the boards, executives, and medical staff who have helped their organizations achieve the highest level of performance nationwide over the most recent five-year period.[4] To top it off, *Georgia Trend Magazine* in December 2010 reported that Health-Grades Inc. ranked NGHS first in two out of eight clinical areas considered, and second in two more. These accomplishments are the result of the outstanding efforts of the entire health system staff and hospital community, but special credit must go to the senior leaders for their commitment to continuous personal and organizational improvement. Their leadership made a difference.

NGHS is one of many organizations that have validated the continuous development approach. Just as a screw or an auger provides a mechanical advantage with each turn, the Continuous Development Model gives individuals and teams a leadership advantage with each completed circuit. Like a spiral stairway, this model/process allows people and teams to climb higher and higher toward their full potential.

Foot Stomper: Authentic leaders engage in continual development. Knowledge alone is not enough; the only way to grow as a leader is to do things differently, and that requires change. Go first, and then take your people with you.

⑦ Coaching: DEVELOP YOUR PEOPLE

If you want your people to develop, set the example by engaging in ongoing development with them. The best way to lift your organization higher is to take what your team is learning and push it down to the people at the next lower level, so they can then push it down, and so on.

1. **What would be the impact of you and your team leading at a higher level of effectiveness?** How would it affect your time management? How would it affect your communications, decision-making, execution, and accountability?

2. **What should you and your team be working on now?** Like most world-class performers, you will probably need a coach. Who will facilitate your development process?

3. **What would be the benefit of ongoing development as a standard practice at every level?** Do you have a vision for that? What would it take to make it happen?

Note: To download an expanded version of these coaching questions for writing your responses, visit LeadingWithHonor.com/Book.

---

[1] After writing several drafts of this chapter, I read *Unbroken*, the best selling book by Laura Hillenbrand about World War II POW Louis Zamperini. He had similar experiences of a sharpened memory during his forty-seven day survival ordeal in a life raft in the middle of the Pacific Ocean.

[2] Lance Sijan was the first graduate of the Air Force Academy to win the Congressional Medal of Honor. Sijan Hall at the Academy is named in his honor. For more on Lance Sijan, read *Into the Mouth of the Cat* by Malcolm McConnell.

[3] "Keys to Profitability: Lessons from Ratios Profit Leaders." *Graphic Arts Monthly*, November 1, 2003.

[4] *NGHS Latest News*, http://www.nghs.com/news.

Chapter 10

BALANCE MISSION AND PEOPLE

"Mission First, People Always"

U.S. Army Slogan

Military leaders have two primary responsibilities: to accomplish the mission and to care for the people. Balancing these two priorities can be difficult in normal times. In a wartime environment, with lives on the line, it can be a gut-wrenching challenge.

First and foremost is the accomplishment of the mission. In other words, job number one is to get the job done. Our mission in the air war was to stop the flow of supplies and troops from North Vietnam into South Vietnam. In support of this overall objective, I flew more than seventy combat missions (sorties) in Southeast Asia, and I was on my fifty-third mission over North Vietnam when shot down.

When I was captured, my mission immediately switched from offense to defense. The new objectives were to survive, to support my comrades, and to prevent the enemy from exploiting me in any way that would undermine the U.S. government and its war efforts. Stripped of my sidearm and my once-elegant flying machine, now scattered across hostile terrain, my only weapons were my mind, body, and spirit. I had experienced very realistic S.E.R.E (survival, evasion, resistance, and escape) training, so I understood my new mission, but I had no idea what sacrifices it would entail.

Early in the war, our POW leaders distilled our mission to six powerful words: "resist, survive, and return with honor." Eventually, it was shortened to just "return with honor." This short expression provided clear guidance, strong motivation, and benchmarks for measuring success. Although we desperately wanted to return home, returning in shame was an unthinkable option.[1]

As mentioned earlier, the Military Code of Conduct (see Appendix

B) provided the practical framework for leading and serving with honor. Its six brief articles containing only 250 words provide broad guidance for virtually every scenario POWs face. First tested under fire in the Vietnam War, it proved to be an amazing document that clarified expected behaviors and set the boundaries for our resistance strategies.[2]

We found that the Code of Conduct had to be interpreted in light of the specific circumstances. How long should a person resist under torture before completing a biography or agreeing to read the propaganda news into a tape recorder to be played over the camp radio? Under what conditions should we try to escape? How much torture should someone take to avoid meeting with a peace delegation? These were not hypothetical issues that a detached executive in a remote, top-floor corner office would address for implementation by the rank and file. In the POW camps, the decision-makers knew they were likely to be the first to follow their own guidance.

Risner, Stockdale, and Denton had made it clear that we were to refuse to participate in propaganda broadcasts. But under extreme torture, it was impossible to totally resist. As we learned from the experience of several men who did not come home, at some point mind, body, and spirit break, causing loss of rational/coherent thought and the ability to effectively function. Therefore, Risner further clarified this policy by adding that we should "take torture indefinitely, but stop short of losing life or limb or mental facilities by falling back to a second line of defense." Having been pushed beyond his endurance several times, he knew that sometimes temporary submission was the only way to preserve the ability to fight.

Because some POWs were simply tougher mentally and physically than others, local SROs had the freedom to interpret resistance policies to suit the circumstances. Major Larry Guarino (USAF), who heroically stood up to some of the worst treatment during the darkest days at the Zoo Camp, demonstrated wise discernment about how to effectively balance accomplishment of mission and care for the men. He said, "There are wide differences in people. A very few men, like Jim Kasler

{Major, USAF} have the stamina and courage to stick to a hard line during severe punishment and continue to hold out. Most men, although they want to do a good job, will gamely resist the cruelties, but not for very long." [3]

Although our leaders were often tortured first and most, they did not pretend to be macho "John Wayne" heroes. On the contrary, they openly shared the pain and despair of their brokenness, helping us understand the enemy's tactics and the realities of what was and was not possible.[4] It would have been disastrous for the mission and for their credibility had they been less than totally honest with us about their experiences in the torture chambers. Mutual accountability and transparency in the face of a cruel enemy bonded us tightly together.

An analysis conducted after the war by Headquarters USAF reflects the sacrifices and commitment made to achieve the mission:[5]

- Nine faithful warriors died before they could return with honor. We lost eight brave men due to extreme torture and deprivation in the earlier years, and one died of typhoid fever.

- More than 95 percent of POWs were tortured.

- Approximately 40 percent of POWs were in solitary confinement for more than six months; 20 percent were in solitary for more than a year; 10 percent were in solitary for more than two years; and several were in solitary more than four years.

Considering the length of stay and the crowded conditions, our survival record was remarkable. Most of us made it back, and our mental and emotional state exceeded the predictions of most of the mental health professionals advising DOD.[6]

The overall determination and devotion of this group to our mission was impressive. Of the nearly five hundred POWs in our network, fewer than ten (2 percent) willingly cooperated with the enemy.

In these cases, our leaders meted out discipline, which could include denial of SRO status. Capt Ken Fisher provided this type of accountability regarding LtCol Minter, as we discussed in Chapter 2.

As we settled into an era of better treatment in 1970, the focus of the mission began to shift from resistance to survival. Most agreed that a belligerent attitude had been helpful to our cause and our psyche during the reign of terror, but when the enemy backed off on exploitation and adopted more of a "live and let live" policy, it was less advantageous to keep poking them in the eye.

Some of our leaders faced challenges from radical "hard liners" who saw it as their (and our) continuing mission to "give 'em hell" at every opportunity. A few men who had been rather timid during the hard times became inappropriately and recklessly brave when punishment was less likely. SROs had to walk a tightrope. They did not want to restrict fellow POWs from expressing their legitimate disdain for the enemy, yet they realized that antagonism could easily cross a line that would bring unnecessary reprisals on everyone in the cell, and even in the entire compound.

When we began living with forty to sixty men jammed into each cell, philosophical disagreements on routine issues of life occasionally ignited rebellious attitudes internally as well. As the V began to loosen their grip, some POWs who wanted more autonomy pushed back against our leaders and the tight command structure of Camp Unity. SROs maintained strict accountability and issued a few reprimands, always as privately as possible. Outside the individual cells, only those who operated the intra-camp "flagged" (secret) communications channel had any knowledge of these situations.

Close confinement for month after month, year after year sometimes caused tempers to flare and harsh words to fly. Most leaders, sensing the unique requirements of our family-like environment, showed extraordinary patience and compassion in dealing with interpersonal conflicts, offering a reminder when needed that our enemy was outside the cell. We were admonished to be quick to judge and manage our own shortcomings, while being tolerant of the faults of others. That would be good advice in any situation, but it was especially needed in captivity, where escape from neither friend nor enemy was an option.

Military leaders are taught to take care of their people, and the troops are taught to take care of their teammates. As we fought for survival against an enemy that was using every means to isolate, divide, and conquer us, we would willingly risk torture to support each other. The healthy took care of the sick, and the brave encouraged those more timid. When one man was down, the others did everything possible to lift him up.

Servant leadership was a way of life. LCDR Render Crayton spent six months in solitary because of his efforts to help save the lives of Smitty Harris and Fred Flom. SROs Risner, Stockdale, Denton, and others constantly pressed the V for better treatment and never hesitated to step into the breach on our behalf. In our cell at Son Tay, SRO Capt Ken Fisher was tortured for standing firm against our captors and for our cell's generally "bad asstitudes," much of which were attributable to Warner, Key, Stier, and me.

Even though the military emphasizes command and control, our SROs typically sought input before making decisions. For example, prior to issuing his famous BACK US policy, Stockdale reviewed his thoughts with cellmate Dan Glenn (LTJG, USN). He valued Dan's counsel, even though he was a relatively new POW. At Son Tay, Ken Fisher always previewed and discussed his decisions with the rest of us. In Unity room 3, SRO Doug Clower routinely consulted with his six flight commanders and invited input from any of us. Thinking back, I am tremendously impressed by the way our leaders listened respectfully to our ideas. When they adopted some of mine, I felt valued far above what my junior ranking merited.

Our tough, results-oriented leaders also showed remarkable compassion toward those who had made mistakes. After we were settled in Camp Unity (the big rooms in the Hanoi Hilton), the senior leaders offered amnesty to some of the weaker men, who earlier had naïvely cooperated with the enemy, on condition that they commit to serving faithfully with us going forward. When some of the hardliners pushed back against this leniency, Risner and other longtime SROs responded by issuing a policy saying, "It is not American or Christian to nag a repentant sinner to his grave." The amnesty stood, and on that basis almost all of the lost sheep came back into the fold. Unfortunately, two black sheep, one of whom was Minter, chose to remain allied with the enemy flock rather than rejoining ours.

The sacrificial service of our SROs continued after our repatriation. Even though they had been away from their families for six, seven, and even eight years, shortly after our return they devoted an entire week to completing formal evaluations describing how every POW had performed during captivity. This unselfish, voluntary, precedent-setting effort made a significant difference in our careers. In my case, it resulted in promotion to the rank of major two years ahead of my peer group.

Like all leaders, the SROs struggled to balance the often-competing demands of accomplishing the mission and caring for the people. Even as they pushed us to risk our welfare by resisting the enemy, they sought to minimize our suffering and injury. Their courage in pursuing the mission and their humility and concern for us under the most trying conditions won our hearts and earned our highest respect.

⑦ LESSON: BALANCE MISSION AND PEOPLE

In civilian organizations, the terms "results" and "relationships" are more common than "mission" and "people," so I'll use them here. If results can be thought of as the *head*, or *logical*, side of leadership, relationships might be thought of as the *heart*, or *feelings*, side. Effective leaders understand that results and relationships, although often in tension, are both essential and complementary. To stay viable, you must get results. To get results, you must build relationships, because the energy and motivation that drive accomplishment comes from the hearts and emotions of people. Let's examine some of the challenges to balancing these two important aspects of leadership.

Get Results

Some leaders are inherently results-oriented. Although they are capable of being compassionate, they naturally are more focused on completing tasks, getting results, and achieving goals than on taking care of people.

Every organization exists for a purpose. If it fails to fulfill that purpose (accomplish its mission), it ultimately will cease to exist. In a very real sense, the business environment is a battlefield upon which life and death struggles are continuously waged.

Responsibility for an organization's successes and failures, and ultimately its survival, falls squarely on the shoulders of its leader. Additionally, leaders who get results attract followers and accrue the power of influence. People want to be part of a winning team.

Results-oriented leaders
- See the big picture and provide vision
- Act decisively and give direction
- Communicate directly and behave in a straightforward manner

- Set high standards and clarify expectations
- Focus on tasks
- Solve problems
- Hold people accountable for their performance and actions

Unfortunately, results-oriented leaders often can be oblivious to the human side of the leadership equation. I witnessed a stark example of this problem when I was called in by the HR department of a division of a Fortune 500 company. A specialized unit of this organization, led by a group of results-oriented superstars, was highly regarded for its record of mission successes (results). Marring this record, however, was a formal complaint that had been filed by a lower-level team member about the organization's "hostile" work environment.

As it turned out, I had known the senior manager earlier in my career as a person of good character. Being especially careful to keep an open mind, I conducted a number of interviews to gain insights into the issues that had caused the complaint. I learned that although no one had been treated unfairly, the extraordinarily high standards of the senior leaders, coupled with their stern accountability for missed goals, had created an extremely tense, demanding, and fearful atmosphere, primarily among the lower-level employees.

Because this unit regularly hosted and provided services to the organization's CEO and other officers, the managers had established higher standards for dress and decorum than were in effect in the rest of the company. Some younger associates at the lower levels did not understand why these "looking sharp" policies were necessary, and they felt unfairly punished when they didn't personally comply. When faced with questions and challenges from below, the leaders made matters worse by applying their natural results-oriented skills with greater intensity.

Prior to conducting a leadership class, I asked members of the senior team to complete a personality assessment. These leaders were fine people with good values, but the test revealed them to be the most results-oriented group I had ever encountered. In fact, when they reviewed their reports, they were stunned to see how much their natural "results" strengths outweighed their "relationship" strengths. They tended to be highly challenging, very direct, and impatient hard-chargers who were generally poor listeners and unaware of the emotions and feelings of others. These tendencies were further exacerbated by their high-pressure, results-oriented work environment.

Don't be too critical of these leaders. Under pressure, we all have a tendency to fall back on our strongest innate traits and familiar habits. If they have served us well in the past, why not turn to them again? Abraham Maslow explained this phenomenon by saying, "If all you have is a hammer, everything looks like a nail."

Results-oriented skills are essential, but they must be balanced with relational skills. If you are naturally results-oriented, adding relational abilities to your leadership repertoire may feel unnatural at first. But acquiring any new skill—whether it's learning to dance, ride a bicycle, or speak a second language—initially feels awkward. So, if you think that you might need additional capabilities in your leadership toolbox, be courageous, lean into the pain, and develop the skills you lack. That's what the leaders of this organization did, and the work environment gradually improved.

Build Relationships

Relationship-oriented leaders instinctively focus on developing and supporting others. Through the natural application of their talents and behaviors, they create environments that cultivate loyalty and allow people to thrive in their work over the long term.

Relationship-oriented leaders
- Listen well
- Show respect for others
- Give encouragement and feedback
- Demonstrate compassion, care, and concern for people
- Trust people to do their jobs

- Support people and lend a helping hand
- Help people develop their talents

Leaders who emphasize relationships motivate and inspire their followers to achieve success, because those behaviors touch the deepest desires of human beings: to be valued, to be respected, to have significance, to make a difference, to be accepted, to be part of a larger purpose, to be in community, to be treated fairly, and to hear "well done." Exercising relationship skills is as natural to these leaders as floating downstream.

However, excessive emphasis on relationships can cause problems. That was certainly the case with a unit of a large company we were called in to help. It didn't take long to come to the conclusion that most of the issues facing this organization's executive team related to the leadership style of the senior manager. He was very popular, but his followers sensed that their unit was losing influence in the company because it was failing to make the desired impact. The more results-oriented members were very frustrated with this leader's lack of vision and decisiveness. Since they lacked any authority to take control, they were mentally and emotionally checking out.

We met with the leader before the scheduled team session to review his personality assessment, which showed that he was strongly people-centered. While discussing his profile and the struggles of his team, he suddenly exclaimed, "I think I see the problem: it's me. I gravitate toward relational things, and I dislike dealing with some of the tougher issues like clarifying next steps, setting deadlines, and competing for funding in the company. I want to keep everyone happy and avoid conflict, so I try to get 100 percent agreement on every issue, and I don't hold people accountable for timely results."

Needless to say, we were impressed with this manager's remarkable honesty, humility, and insight. And I was equally impressed with his subsequent efforts toward becoming a better-rounded leader. Although changing his style took time and effort, he made enough progress to turn his team around and become more viable in the organization.

In the process, he learned to better use the talents of the more results-oriented people around him.

Over a period of years, I surveyed more than three hundred managers to find out what traits were present in the leaders they identified as outstanding. Two important insights emerged:

- Although all survey participants acknowledged the importance of achieving results, the great majority said they remembered their best leaders more for their relationship skills. In fact, even among those who considered themselves primarily "results-oriented," 80 percent identified a relationship skill from the list above as the most outstanding characteristic of their best leader.

- A willingness to listen was the leadership trait people respected most in their leaders.

Even the best relationship skills cannot keep everyone satisfied, because relationships alone do not satisfy. People want and need to achieve worthwhile goals. They desire leaders who will establish boundaries and exhibit the tough love that they sometimes need to grow and excel. Effective leaders are always working both sides of the equation to meet the seemingly competing needs of mission and people.

Balancing Results and Relationships

If people were computers or machines, leaders could focus entirely on results and push their followers 24/7 to achieve maximum output. But as Ken Blanchard and Marc Muchnick so well illustrate in their fable, *The Leadership Pill: The Missing Ingredient in Motivating People Today*, focusing entirely on achievement succeeds only for a short period. If prolonged, it will actually hinder results. On the other hand, a more balanced approach that focuses on results and people allows organizations to reach their fullest potential.

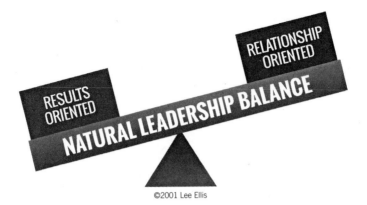

©2001 Lee Ellis

Most people are naturally more talented on one side than the other.
Working toward a balanced approach can significantly improve
your leadership effectiveness.

Leaders who balance the competing demands of results and relationships are able to push for the achievement of goals, while eliciting
the best from their people. It's as if they have two bank accounts. They
make deposits in their "results" account by consistently accomplishing
their goals, and they build up capital in their "relationship" account
by caring for their people as individuals of worth. In the first instance
they earn credibility with their superiors, and in the second they earn
loyalty from their followers.

Occasionally leaders will need to make withdrawals from these bank
accounts. For example, a leader who is being pressured by unrealistic
expectations from above may need to draw on the credibility she's
accumulated in her "results" bank account and say to her superiors,
"We need to adjust this timetable, or we'll burn out our people."
At other times she may have to make a withdrawal from the relationship bank account and say to her team, "We'll have to work over the
weekend to get this job done."

With regard to balancing mission and people, Admiral Stockdale
wisely said, "A leader must remember that he is responsible for his
charges. He must tend his flock, not only cracking the whip, but 'washing their feet' when they are in need of help."[7]

Balancing "results and relationships" is a major leadership challenge. Some leaders are naturally gifted with the head (logic) and not very good with the heart (feelings). Others are just the opposite. Only about 20 percent of the population has a natural ability with both. Even those with this "tightrope-walking" capability often end up tilting toward a results-oriented style, because results are typically what get noticed and rewarded.

If your leadership style is unbalanced, the good news is that you don't have to reinvent yourself. (That would be impossible anyway!) To gain better balance, you simply have to develop some of the skills you lack. Put simply, you may either need to "toughen up" or "soften up." This may sound artificial, but with practice your adapted behaviors will feel more comfortable. They will never become totally natural, however, so you'll have to consistently and intentionally work at keeping your balance.

Most leaders can dramatically increase their effectiveness by simply gaining a better balance between results and relationships. Use this framework as you observe your own leadership and the styles of others. Becoming more aware of this dynamic will enable you to coach yourself into a better balance that will result in a higher level of performance.[8]

Foot Stomper: Outstanding leaders balance accomplishment of the mission (results) *and* care for their people (relationships). However, the styles of most leaders are naturally biased toward one end of the spectrum or the other. To enhance your leadership effectiveness, find out which types of skills you need to develop. Then, leaning into the pain of your doubts and fears, adapt your behaviors to do what you know a good leader should do.

⑦ Coaching: BALANCE MISSION AND PEOPLE

Do you tilt toward *results* or *relationships*? If you're unsure, look at the list of strengths for each in this chapter and see which feels more natural and comfortable for you. Or, for a more comprehensive look, you may want to complete the online *Leadership Behavior DNA™* Assessment (see page 234 for a free offer). It will provide insights into your leadership strengths, so you'll know whether you tend to favor results or relationships.[9]

1. **How can you develop your leadership balance?** Once you know your natural traits, identify two behaviors (skills) from the other list in this chapter that you could work on to better balance your leadership style. For example if you are naturally results-oriented, skills in that list will come easy. To gain a better balance look at the list of relationship-oriented skills and select two that you could work on to gain a better balance in your leadership.

2. **What will be the payoff to you if you learn to use these new leadership behaviors?** When will you begin practicing your new behaviors?

3. **What would be the impact if all your leaders gained a better balance of results and relationships (mission and people)?** How could you make that happen?

Note: To download an expanded version of these coaching questions for writing your responses, visit LeadingWithHonor.com/Book.

---

[1] Jamie Howren and Taylor Baldwin Kiland, "Vietnam POWs Thirty Years Later," http://www.opendoorsbook.com/message.php (accessed April 6, 2011).

[2] Robert K. Rule, "The Code of Conduct," http://www.au.af.mil/au/awc/awcgate/au-24/ruhl.pdf (accessed October 12, 2010).

[3] Larry Guarino, *A POW's Story: 2801 Days in Hanoi.* (New York, NY: Ballantine Books, 1990) 166.

[4] Shortly after our release, President Nixon hosted the POWs at the White House for the largest Gala ever held there. Hollywood stars sat at each table. Colonel Larry Guarino told his table host, actor John Wayne, that initially he had responded to the V like he thought John Wayne would have. Duke asked him, "What happened?" Guarino responded, "They beat the s__t out of me." His response brought tears to Duke's eyes. Guarino, 165.

[5] HQ USAF/XOX Study, *SEAsia PW Analysis Program Report*, Washington DC, 1974.

[6] Two months after our release, I met with Holocaust survivor and Psychiatrist Dr. Victor Frankl who had served on a Department of Defense Advisory Board consulting on what to expect on our release. He said, "Many of my colleagues were very worried, but I told them you would be okay."

[7] James B. Stockdale, *Thoughts of a Philosophical Fighter Pilot*. (Stanford University, CA: Hoover Institution Press, 1995).

[8] Lee Ellis, "*What is Your Leadership Balance?*" LeadingWithHonor.com/Balance.

[9] "*Leadership Behavior DNA™,*" (see page 234 for a free offer).

Chapter 11

BUILD COHESIVE TEAMS

★

"Coming together is a beginning.
Keeping together is progress.
Working together is success."

Henry Ford

At every turn the V sought to exploit us for their cause by undermining our leadership structure and our teamwork. We were alert to their tactics and circled the wagons. The remarkable unity among our leaders set a positive tone in the camps and laid the foundation for good teamwork at lower levels. There was no evidence of bickering and petty politics among our senior leaders.

As with any military unit, we had clear lines of authority and a prearranged succession plan based on date of rank, so disputes never arose about who was in charge. When one SRO was pulled out of the cellblock for isolation or torture, the next ranking leader stepped up and carried on without missing a beat. Nevertheless, the V constantly attempted by various means to weaken our chain of command. For example, if everyone in a cell had the rank of captain or lieutenant, they might put a major in the room who seemed to them to be more compliant. This never worked, because even the more "user friendly" officers held the line against the enemy.

The V also tried to undermine our teamwork by selecting a junior officer to represent the cell and telling the rest of us that we could only work through him. In other words, they attempted to determine our leaders for us. To combat this tactic, the junior officer would tell the guard or interrogator that he would pass the message to his SRO, and that the SRO would respond. Our passive-aggressive tactics wore down the V, and before long they again addressed issues to the SRO in proper fashion. Military training and discipline enabled us to maintain clear lines of authority, which kept us aligned and helped minimize any disruptive cliques or splinter groups.

Teamwork requires trust, coupled with a sacrificial commitment to each other. When Jon Reynolds refused to make a propaganda statement, the V cut off his food ration and moved him to a cell that was pitch dark all day and brightly lit all night. When this "slow torture" failed to break him, they beat him until he relented. After the V had extracted a forced "statement," they took Reynolds back to his old cell, but they still gave him no food.

"Percy" Purcell, an old fighter pilot friend of Jon's, happened to be in a neighboring cell. When he heard about Jon's deplorable condition, Percy sent a message via tap code across several cells: "Stand by for a piece of bread in the early afternoon."

Jon couldn't imagine how Percy would fulfill his promise. But sure enough, after the noon hour, when most of the guards were taking their afternoon siestas, dust and dirt began falling from around the single light bulb in the ceiling of Jon's cell. The bulb and wire dropped down a couple of feet, and some slender pieces of stale bread appeared, like manna from heaven. It was the first food Jon had seen in eight days. A grinning Percy peered through the hole, offered a few words of encouragement, and scampered back through the attic before the guards discovered his absence. The likelihood of being caught was high, and the consequences would have been severe. Percy's feat to help a fellow POW is regarded by his peers as one of the most courageous acts of teamwork during our experience.

Our commitment to each other transcended race and other differences. The V, well aware of some of the racial issues in the United States, put Navy LTJG Porter Halyburton, a white man who had grown up in segregated North Carolina, in a cell with Major Fred Cherry, a black man reared in segregated Virginia. They even reminded Cherry of how the white man had exploited him and other blacks. Cherry saw through their schemes and did not take the bait.

Although Halyburton's family had enjoyed close relationships with African-Americans, he had never been under the authority of a black person, so it felt to him a little strange. Moreover, since he had never seen a black pilot, he was initially suspicious that Cherry might be a spy. To Halyburton's credit as an officer and a person, he quickly realized that the major was a legitimate teammate. He became Cherry's personal servant as well as a loyal follower.

Major Cherry was so badly wounded—he suffered from a separated shoulder, a broken arm, and a broken leg, among other injuries—that he couldn't eat, bathe, or go to the toilet by himself. Without constant care, it was only a matter of time before he would have died. For six months Halyburton completely attended to Cherry's every need, nursing him back to the point where the major could care for himself. This story, which was widely known among POWs, has been documented in James Hirsch's excellent book *Two Souls Indivisible: The Friendship That Saved Two Lives in Vietnam.*[1]

After years of living in small rooms of one to eight men, teamwork took on a new dimension when we were moved back to the Hanoi Hilton after the Son Tay raid. Although most of the fifty-five of us cooped up in room 3 had never met face-to-face, we knew each other's names and we had been in many of the same camps. To promote teamwork and cohesion, our SRO organized us into six flights, each led by the six next senior ranking officers in the cell.

Our common mindset about living and working together significantly strengthened our teamwork. We understood the importance of maintaining mutual respect, and we accepted each other's differences, even those habits and personality quirks that annoyed us. Herded together in such close quarters without the possibility of escaping to solitude, little things like the noises people make when they blow their noses or clear their throats would grate on our nerves.

We synchronized our daily lives, much like a dance group would synchronize a performance. At bedtime mosquito nets went up and people quieted down for the evening. In the morning around 6:30, mosquito nets came down and the floor around the elevated sleeping platform was cleared for walking. We had regular procedures for meals, educational classes, and other activities that allowed us to function without getting in each other's way.

Even though we were all aircrews serving in the military, we were a very diverse cross-section of the American culture. Some of us had grown up in the city and some in the country; some came from poverty and some from wealth. Most of us were protestant or Catholic, and a few of us were Jewish.

Faith in God and faith in country were extremely important and were often interwoven into our daily lives and practices. Religious observances focused our attention on a higher purpose and cultivated relationship-strengthening attitudes like humility, kindness, and forgiveness. In the early years when we were in small rooms of one to four men, church was held shortly after the morning meal each Sunday. The compound or cellblock SRO initiated services by sending the coded signal V V, short for "Victory in Vietnam." Each cell responded by conducting their own version of church. Most included the "Lord's Prayer," a memorized selection from the Psalms, and a time for private prayer. It was common to conclude our services by reciting the Pledge of Allegiance.

It was a Sunday church service that elicited the most unifying and dramatic event of our POW experience. The Hanoi "church riot" occurred about three months after the panic move back to the Hanoi Hilton when we were jammed into seven larger rooms. Emboldened by our numbers, we began for the first time to flex our muscles. In direct violation of the V's policies, on February 7, 1971, Robbie Risner, assisted by CDR Howie Rutledge and LTJG George Coker, conducted a planned church service for room seven. The "congregation" was composed mainly of tough senior officers and some of the most "die hard" resistors in the camp.

The V, furious at this defiance of their authority, hauled Risner and his two assistants off to solitary confinement and torture in Heartbreak Hotel. As they were being led away, Major Bud Day jumped up on the sleeping platform and began singing "The Star Spangled Banner." The entire room burst into song. A few moments later, singing erupted from room six, then from room five and on down the line, until more than three hundred voices were exulting without inhibition from all seven rooms. The proud strains rang out over the fifteen-foot walls of the camp and reverberated outside in the streets of downtown Hanoi.

Risner heard the singing as he was being escorted away, and his spirits soared. It is an honor to serve with men like these, he thought, straightening his back and lifting his head with pride. Years later, after Risner returned home, someone asked him how he felt on that day when he heard the singing continue. He replied, "I felt like I was nine feet tall and could whip a bear with a switch."[2]

The "church riot" was so exhilarating that later in the afternoon men in room seven started singing "God Bless America." Maj Larry Guarino yelled out, "This is building seven, building seven, building seven, this is building number seven. Where the hell is building six?" Of course, room six picked up the chant, which was then passed from room to room all around the compound to room one. The V panicked, but this time they were ready. The doors to all rooms were flung open and squads of troops—complete with hard hats, fixed bayonets and tear gas—entered each cell. That was the end of the infamous Hanoi "church riot," but not to our resistance to the no-church policy.

The leaders in room seven were not intimidated. Over the next week, nine consecutive SROs were removed and put in isolation as a result of the ongoing battle with the V. In the end, the enemy yielded and allowed us to conduct regular formal church services. The increased unity that resulted from the church riot boosted our morale and helped us persevere over the next two years as we awaited repatriation. It also established the name of the compound: "Camp Unity."

We constantly asked for a Bible, but the V, who were terrified of religion, always denied having any. We suspected—and later learned—that our families had sent stacks of them. Eventually our captors allowed two men per cell to access a Bible for an hour on Saturdays. Our designated scribes would copy a chapter or two using paper and pencil the V provided, and we would later memorize some passages and use them in our services.

Conflict is inevitable in life, and we had our share of it inside the cells and across the camp. If you have a healthy team (good trust and cohesion), conflict works to your advantage and makes you stronger and more effective. Before making some of the more controversial decisions, our leaders allowed—and even facilitated—passionate debate.

Much of our "creative conflict" in the camps over the years focused on an article of the Code of Conduct that said a POW should make every effort to escape. Some men interpreted this to mean that we should always be working on escape plans. Others argued that in our location and situation, escape attempts were likely to fail, and even if successful for a few, they wouldn't be worth the cost for others.

The debate became especially passionate after two men attempted to escape from the Zoo Camp and were quickly recaptured. Both were so severely tortured that one died. The men living in the same and adjoining buildings were tortured for weeks—some nearly to death—until the V learned all the details of the plot. POWs throughout all the camps were under the gun for several months. As mentioned earlier, many were tortured just because they were doing something that aroused suspicion.[3] Risner and the senior officers in Camp Unity listened to arguments on both sides of the escape debate and issued an order that we would only attempt escape if we had outside help. Still, there were always covert groups working on contingency plans.

Because we had so little leverage over the V, many of our leadership conflicts arose over the efficacy of punishing ourselves in order to punish the enemy. For example, by 1970 the campaign for better treatment from our families and others back home had made our captors more sensitive to world opinion. Although they were still using isolation and occasional beatings to punish us, we sensed that they wanted to keep us relatively healthy and happy to boost their image if and when we were released. This gave us some leverage, but ironically we had to punish ourselves to use it.

With few options at our disposal, some POWs proposed a hunger strike to pressure the V into improving our conditions. Debate on this issue was serious and passionate. Those opposed argued that men who were in poor health could not survive long without food. Eventually,

SRO Denton gave the order for a partial fast, but he called it off after a short time because many of the men were wilting away.

John McCain came up with an idea that seemed more feasible, but was almost as controversial. By the spring of 1971, again for public relations purposes, the V were eagerly encouraging us to write a seven-line letter home about once a month. McCain proposed that if we suddenly quit writing, the people back home would assume we were being treated more harshly and would intensify their calls for better treatment.[4] Perhaps this high-risk game of chicken would even precipitate a visit to the camp by the Red Cross.

Some liked this idea, but others disagreed on the grounds that a writing moratorium would unnecessarily punish families and heighten their anxiety about our circumstances. Across the camp men debated the pros and cons of this proposal, and the summaries of room discussions were relayed to the command section. After thoughtful consideration, the senior staff decided in favor of the moratorium, but made it optional.

Within a few months, most had joined the boycott. We had no means of measuring the effectiveness of this initiative, which lasted almost six months. Its most impressive aspect was the unity it fostered when more than three hundred strong-willed POWs voluntarily bore such a significant sacrifice. Judicious debate on the front end allowed all sides to be heard and resulted in high buy-in to a very controversial strategy.

In retrospect, the overall cohesion among POWs was impressive. To be sure, there were some people who just did not get along, but when you consider the close living conditions, the strong personalities, and the controversial issues that frequently arose, we stayed committed to each other. My fifty-five teammates in room 3 of Camp Unity probably held the record for unity. In the nineteen months that we lived together, there were only two times when someone yelled at another person in anger. In both cases, they settled their issues before bedtime that evening. That experience provided a great lesson in cohesion that has served me well.

⑦ LESSON: BUILD COHESIVE TEAMS

Cohesive teamwork is built on trust, which developed rather quickly in the "us against them" crucible of the camps. Building trust in normal environments requires more time, work, and intentionality. At Leadership Freedom we use a combination of several team-building models and interactive exercises to illustrate and expedite the process. We begin by emphasizing that teams are composed of unique individuals, and that our differences typically push us apart. Then we consider what needs to be the same, and what can—and possibly should be—different. The chart below provides a good framework for clarifying how unity and diversity work together.

Unity and Diversity

Same	Different
• Mission	• Talents
• Commitment	• Motivations
• Organizational values	• Ideas/Interests
• Opportunity/Loyalty	• Needs
• Policies/Discipline	• Styles

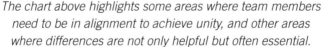

The chart above highlights some areas where team members need to be in alignment to achieve unity, and other areas where differences are not only helpful but often essential.

The areas that need to be in the "Same" column will vary depending on the organization, so it is important for leaders to clarify what is essential for unity. The goal is to clarify the minimum framework for cohesion—the Same column—while allowing as much freedom as possible for people to be different, thus maximizing the advantages of diversity.

I like to use personality assessments in team development, because they provide an understandable, nonthreatening tool for discussing differences and diversity.[5] When people can see differences expressed with scientifically derived graphs and numbers that are associated with specific strengths and struggles, they begin to appreciate that differences are natural, necessary, and beneficial for most teams. This understanding helps each individual own his or her personal strengths and struggles, and genuinely value the strengths and struggles of others. (See Appendix D for a *Leadership Behavior DNA*™ Comparison Graph showing differences.)

Building cohesive teamwork requires *understanding* and *acceptance*, but that's not easy. Our natural tendency is to judge "different" as wrong. Instead of appreciating differences, we get irritated at them. Think about it: If you are decisive, how do you react to teammates who seem to take forever to make a decision? If you are reserved, do you find nonstop talkers exhausting and annoying? And if you are neat, organized, and always on time, how do you feel about people who are habitually late, forgetful, messy, and disorganized?

As a good teammate, you need to realize that you are not going to change another person's natural struggles, so you might as well accept them. Learn to value their strengths, which are invariably present in greater abundance than their struggles. Allow people to utilize their strengths, which are different from yours, to complement your struggles, which are different from theirs. Your *respect* for others will grow as you focus on their positives and take ownership of your struggles.

Humility and transparency build *trust*, which is the glue of team cohesion. Throughout this process, good *communications* and mutual *commitment* to one another provide the guardrails to keep the team-development process on track.

With trust and cohesion in place, a team is equipped to engage in the creative conflict that is essential for healthy teamwork. That may sound counterintuitive, so let me explain.

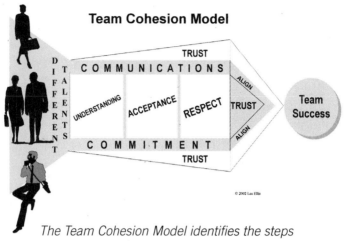

*The Team Cohesion Model identifies the steps
in the team development process.*

Without passionate discussions (creative conflict), team members will have little commitment to decisions. Without commitment to decisions, there will be little ownership and mutual accountability. And without ownership and accountability, teams will work less effectively together, and results will suffer. Patrick Lencioni introduced this progression and the idea of "creative conflict" in *The Five Dysfunctions of a Team,*[6] a widely used source for development. We have used his model and process for years, and I highly recommend it for your teambuilding efforts.

If a team has enough trust and cohesion to engage in creative conflict, it can work through almost any challenge. I have seen some of the biggest organizational breakthroughs come after teams developed this skill.

In Chapter 9, I described the successes of the leadership team of Northeast Georgia Hospital System (NGHS). Following the team-development process described above, they focused on getting comfortable with creative conflict. Initially it helped them work in cross-functional teams to reduce their budget by twenty million dollars, thereby improving their financials. Amazingly, they came out of that exercise stronger and more unified.

Now, several years later, the leaders are so at ease with passionate dialog that an outsider might think they are at war with each other. In fact, they are careful to alert new team members and staff-meeting visitors in advance, so they won't be alarmed at the rigorous debate. Observers are surprised that a team can fight so hard and still care about each other so much. But it's exactly this process that bonds the team together in mutual commitment and accountability, resulting in its enviable record of awards and high rankings.

I'm convinced that the true health of a team can be judged by the ability of participants to deal with conflict in a positive way. When people walk on eggshells—afraid to disagree and unwilling to acknowledge "the elephant in the room"—domination and control supplant dialog and cohesion. This takes us back to the obvious but often ignored fact that responsibility for fostering teamwork and achieving results rests with the leader. Sometimes teams succeed in spite of the leader, but the energy required can cause team members to burn out.

To be honest, building cohesive teamwork is not the kind of challenge that most results-oriented leaders enjoy, because it focuses more on the relationship skills that feel "soft and fluffy" to people who are less "emotional." Moreover, developing teamwork may seem like a waste of time to a leader who doesn't fully appreciate the power of cohesion.

While attending the Air War College, I came across some interesting World War II research. It indicated that units could be defeated without being utterly destroyed if enough of the unit was put out of action to break cohesion. Since then, the word *cohesion* has always grabbed my attention. The dictionary defines it as "the act or state of sticking together tightly; *especially*: unity".[7] Sounds powerful, doesn't it!

Foot Stomper: Build trust by helping teammates gain understanding, acceptance, and respect for each other. The resulting unity and cohesion will enable them to engage in creative conflict, which in turn will build the commitment and loyalty necessary to overcome the most difficult challenges.

⑦ Coaching: BUILD COHESIVE TEAMS

Having a cohesive team sounds great, but fostering that level of trust and commitment requires intentional effort. Reflect on these questions to evaluate and improve your current level of cohesion.

1. **What is your current level of cohesion?** What are the evidences of understanding, acceptance, respect, trust, commitment, and unity on your team? What actions could you take to increase cohesion?

2. **What is your capacity to deal with conflict?** Do you feel uncomfortable with expressed emotions and passionate debate? Do you squelch disagreement, perhaps because you feel less respected and less powerful when your ideas are challenged? What are the sources of your fears and what would it take for you to move beyond your discomfort?

3. **What is the ability of your team to engage in creative conflict?** Does your team avoid passionate debate? Do your people leave meetings with less than total buy-in to your decisions? If you answered yes to these questions, you are missing the benefits and fun of leading a cohesive, synergistic team. I encourage you to get a consultant or coach to help you with team development.

Note: To download an expanded version of these coaching questions for writing your responses, visit LeadingWithHonor.com/Book.

---

[1] There were three African Americans in our long-term Hanoi Hilton system cohort; two more joined us late in the war. All were highly respected by their peers. There was never any racial discord.

[2] Ross Perot heard this story and in 2001 sponsored a nine-foot statue of Risner that is a popular attraction at the Air Force Academy. A photo of Risner at the dedication of this statue can be seen at LeadingWithHonor.com/gallery.

[3] We did not know about the escape at the Zoo, but shortly after it occurred, cellmate and would-be scientist Jim Warner was pouring a few drops of water on the back window bars, hoping to grow some moss. The guard saw him and reported it to the camp authorities. The V believed that Jim was trying to escape, and tortured him to find out his plan. Jim had to make up a story; unfortunately he said he would go through the ceiling, which was

exactly what Dramesi and Atterberry had done at the Zoo. Warner spent the next six months in solitary confinement in the tank, a miserably hot little building near the guard shack.

[4] John Hubbell, *POW: A Definitive History of the American Prisoner-of-War Experience in Vietnam*, 1964-1973. (New York, NY: The Readers Digest Press, 1976) 551-552.

[5] You can build cohesion without using personality instruments, but it will take much longer. The process described here typically takes one day, with regular discussions by the team and quarterly facilitation. This process can expedite team cohesion by six months.

[6] Patrick Lencioni, *Overcoming the Five Dysfunctions of a Team: A Field Guide for Leaders, Managers, and Facilitators.* (San Francisco, CA: Jossey Bass, 2005).

[7] *Merriam-Webster Dictionary*, s.v. "Cohesion," http://www.merriam-webster.com/dictionary/cohesion (November 28, 2010).

Chapter 12

EXPLOIT CREATIVITY

*"Imagination is more important
than knowledge."*

Albert Einstein

I didn't know Army LTC Ben Purcell while I was in Vietnam, because he and other POWs captured in South Vietnam were held in different camps. We are both from North Georgia, however, and after the war we became good friends. That's when I learned the details of his fascinating story.

As the executive officer of the 80th General Support Group serving the five provinces of South Vietnam, Purcell often travelled by helicopter from one unit to the next. On one such mission his chopper was hit by ground fire and crashed. He and the four other men aboard were captured. As they were being marched north, one of the men was too severely injured to keep up, so the V pulled him aside. A shot was heard. Purcell and the other three men never saw their companion again.

After two months of travel on foot and by truck, Ben and his three comrades were deposited at a camp in the environs of a city, which they suspected was Hanoi. From outside the walls of the compound came the sounds of trains, vehicles, and people. The V accused Purcell of being a CIA agent, threatened to try him as a war criminal, and told him he may never go home. Alone in solitary confinement, he thought constantly about how desperately his wife, Ann, and their five children needed him. He decided he had to escape and get home to his family.

Ben tricked a guard into divulging that they were indeed ten kilometers south of Hanoi. He hatched a scheme to escape from his cell by removing a panel in the door. He then planned to climb over the camp wall using a rope ladder he would make. Once outside the compound, he would follow the railroad tracks to the city, find the French consulate, and request political asylum.

Every POW talked about escape, but few attempted it. Purcell knew the odds were heavily stacked against him. He did not speak the language; he didn't know the culture; and he didn't look anything like the Asian citizens of the metropolitan area that surrounded the camp. Nevertheless, with determination and ingenuity, he put his plan into action.

To remove the panel, Ben needed a drill. Taking a wire that held his mosquito net to the wall, he sharpened it into a drill bit by rubbing it back and forth on the concrete floor. He then fashioned a handle for his drill by wrapping the dull end of the wire around a small piece of bamboo. Next, he drilled holes around the edges of the panel—he figured it would take about two hundred to provide sufficient perforation—and filled them with a paste made of moistened breadcrumbs and a bit of toothpaste. Finally, he camouflaged each hole by coloring the paste with soot from his lantern to match the gray door. The sawdust went into his toilet bucket, which he emptied daily.

Ben needed a sharp instrument to cut or punch out the pieces of wood between the drill holes, so he extracted a six-penny nail from the wall and flattened its pointed end into a chisel. Then he fabricated a handle for the chisel from pieces of bread dough, which he wrapped around the nail one layer at a time, hardening each layer with the heat of his kerosene lantern. He had to work slowly and cautiously to avoid detection. One day he noticed that a chicken he had occasionally fed with tiny bits of stale bread or rice squawked and ran off whenever the guards came near. Ben started feeding the chicken more often, so he would stay close to his cell. With his "watchchicken" in place, he could work more aggressively.

After three months, Ben was ready. He had drilled a sufficient number of holes to weaken the panel, and he had converted a canvas duffle bag into a ladder, a map case, and a cap that resembled those worn by Vietnamese officers. On the night of December 7, 1969, after a short prayer, he removed the panel, crawled through the door of his cell, sneaked across the camp, climbed up his ladder and over the wall, and raced into the woods.

Then things started to go awry. In the misty night, made even darker by the blackout the V had imposed to avoid air attacks, he couldn't find the railroad tracks. After crisscrossing the terrain several times, he eventually ended up back at the camp. Realizing that sunrise was approaching and that every soldier in the area would soon be looking for him, his only choice was to travel by road.

So here comes Ben, a six-foot American POW, walking down the road to Hanoi wearing his homemade hat and his prison uniform turned inside out. His heart was beating like a loud drum. When no one paid him any attention, he began to think that he was really going to make it. Then a man riding a bicycle stopped to check him out. Looking the bicyclist straight in the eye and trying desperately not to act scared, Ben said in French, "Can you take me to the French consulate?" The man replied, "*Oui*," motioned for Ben to climb on the rear-mounted carrier, and commenced peddling in broad daylight down this road crowded with scurrying Vietnamese.

On the outskirts of Hanoi, the fellow pedaled up to a small building that looked like a carnival booth. It turned out to be a police station. Within an hour, Ben was back in prison, where he was locked down in leg stocks and fed bread and water for thirty days.

After three years of isolation, the V moved Purcell to another camp with more room and much better living conditions. He was watched carefully due to his previous escape attempt, but that did not stop him from contemplating another try. One evening, when the guard came around for the nightly body count, Ben happened to be using the small toilet in the back of his room.[1] The guard quickly moved on to the next cell.

That gave him an idea: he would use his ingenuity to design a urinating dummy. Over the next several weeks, Ben set the stage for his escape by timing his toilet visits to coincide with the nightly body count. During this period, he fashioned a dummy (nicknamed Charley) from some of his belongings and used a rubber bucket the V had left in his cell for the bladder. He punched a hole in the bucket, plugged it, and filled it with water. When he pulled the plug, the water poured down into the toilet bucket, making the same sound as a man urinating. The water flowed for about twenty-five minutes, which would be long enough for him to get out of the camp.

When the night of the planned escape arrived, Ben set the dummy in position, pulled the plug on the rubber bucket, unhooked the barbwire stretched across the transom over his door, and climbed onto a framing board just under the roofline. Fortunately, the guard in the corner tower had vacated his post for supper, so he scampered unseen to the bamboo fence and slithered through a ditch that went underneath. When the guard conducted the body count, he evidently saw the shoulders of the urinating dummy, thought it was Ben, and kept walking. Charley had done his job, and Ben got his twenty-five minutes of escape time to get away from the camp. But within a few hours, Purcell could hear chaotic noises of approaching search parties. After eluding them for eighteen hours, he unfortunately walked right into a cadre of armed guards.

Although Ben's escapes were not successful, the planning and innovation kept his mind occupied and gave him a sense of achievement. During the remainder of his captivity, he continued to exercise his creativity by fashioning a number of items, including a tiny communion set that he made from empty aluminum toothpaste tubes and some buttons that he carved from bones he found in his soup. Purcell lived in solitary confinement for most of his five years as a POW, but his ingenuity and escape attempts gave him the self-respect and confidence he needed to resist, survive, and return with honor.

An extraordinary amount of ingenuity and talent bubbled up in all the POW camps. Navy LT Dan Glenn, who had a degree in architecture, spent several months designing a home. He drew the floor plan and the external renderings using ink he formulated out of brick dust, ashes, and various other materials he found in his cell. He then took sheets of toilet paper, which resembled brown paper towels, and layered them into cardboard-like sheets using glue he made from rice paste. Next, he cut out pieces of this "cardboard" using a contraband razor blade and glued them together to make a scale model of the house. Finally, he painted the model using paints he created from materials around the room. It looked just like a model you would see in an architect's office. Dan designed several houses over the next two years, one of which he actually built and lived in after the war.

Ensign Ralph Gaither, Navy F-4 Pilot, was a man of varied talents. He wrote poetry, sang, played the guitar, and preached with conviction. This courageous resistor was also famous in the camps as a skilled craftsman who could make any tool that a POW might need. His cellmates claimed that the drills Gaither made from pieces of wire were better than those sold in hardware stores back home. They were so precise, in fact, that he even numbered them. For example, the "Gaither number 4" was good for drilling through sixteen-inch concrete walls. Ralph designed and made a mouthpiece from bread dough for one POW that was "better than the $250 one the doctor made back home!"[2] Post Vietnam, he built an experimental aircraft (VariEase) that he flew for more than fifteen years.

Over at the Plantation Camp, Charlie Plumb (LTJG, USN) was the resident inventor. An engineer with a strong background in electronics, he developed more than a dozen devices to measure time, temperature, and weight. He was well on his way to making a radio when the V discovered his stash of razor blades, nails, wire, spools, and tinfoil. Plumb also scratched a keyboard on his bed boards and went over the notes until he could hear them in his head.

As already mentioned, innovation in our communications was so constant it became a way of life. After the Son Tay raid, when we were moved back to the Hanoi Hilton and put in larger cells, the amount of communications traffic increased so much that we had difficulty relaying it from one room to the next. Warner had an idea to solve the problem—with "amoebas." He recruited about a dozen guys. Each was to be responsible for one message, a single packet—or "cell"—of information, just as an amoeba is a one-cell organism.

For example, as I received a silent message via hand code from Tom McNish (1st Lt, USAF) over in room two, I would interpret it aloud to the first amoeba in line. After listening to my translation, he would go to a corner of the room and memorize his "byte." The next amoeba in line would then step up, and we would repeat the process. After each amoeba had memorized his packet of information, he would go to the other end of the room and regurgitate the message to a communicator, who would speak it into the next room through the blanket roll. The amoeba would then get back in line and stand by for another byte download. This creative solution allowed us to significantly increase the volume and accuracy of covert communication passing through our room.

Jerry Venanzi (1st Lt, USAF) was an outgoing chap from New Jersey with extraordinary dramatic talents. After six months of solitary confinement at Son Tay, the sense of isolation was getting to be too much for this extrovert. He remembered a story he had read about a Korean War POW who pretended to lose his mind, so he decided to try the same tactic. The next time the guards let Jerry out of his cell to go to the washroom, he hopped on an imaginary motorcycle, kick-started the engine, and roared off across the compound. As we watched his humorous antics through the cracks in our cell doors, we were rolling on the floor laughing. His authentic pantomime and roaring sound effects were so convincing that we rubbed our eyes to see if he was riding a real motorcycle.

Jerry repeated this charade consistently for a few weeks. Then he embellished the act by pretending he had a pet monkey named Barney. He would get on his motorcycle, help Barney onto the seat behind him, and the two of them would tear off across the compound like a couple of teenagers on a lark. He'd talk to that monkey and play with it as if it was real. After a while, the guards were convinced that Jerry was going crazy, so they took him out of solitary.

One evening after dark we heard the rattling of keys. When the turnkey opened the door, there stood Jerry. He was the first new man to join our five-member cell in two years, and what a great addition he was! As a young teen, Jerry had worked at a movie theater, where he had seen some movies so many times he had them memorized. He would entertain us by retelling movies with extraordinary accuracy, sometimes even acting out the scenes. After we were released, I saw *The Days of Wine and Roses*, and it was exactly the way Jerry had dramatically related it to us back in our cell.

After we moved to Unity we had sufficient talents in that big room to carry out all sorts of entertainment programs. Captain Bill Butler (USAF), our resident French and biology expert, was also a musical whiz and a great teacher. He recruited, trained, and directed a fantastic choir who performed on Sundays and on special occasions, such as our Fourth of July celebrations. Anticipating that we might be together for a few more years and that we would need more singers for major performances, he devised an amazing class to teach the basics of music.

Using a piece of broken brick, Bill drew a keyboard on the concrete slab in one corner of the room. The keys were just large enough for a person to stand on, with the black keys shaded to differentiate them from the white ones. He then had his choir members stand on the keys and make their appropriate sounds. Using his choir like an instrument, he moved them to various keys and had them hum their note to demonstrate the major and minor chords, as well as augmented and diminished variations. This highly creative class aroused considerable interest in music. A few months later Bill organized and conducted a Broadway-style musical, *South Pacific*. It was one of the highlights of the year, giving us some fun and taking our minds off our plight, lifting our spirits for a few days. During tryouts, it was obvious to all—including me—that my singing would not enhance the performance, so I enjoyed it as a spectator from my comfortable seat on the elevated sleeping concrete slab.

Major Gene Smith (USAF) treated us to an innovatively orchestrated rendition of the movie *Grand Prix*. Just prior to deployment several of us had given this movie "two thumbs up" for its beautiful women and fast cars with powerful engines that roared around the track in first-of-its-kind surround-sound realism. Gene recruited and positioned men around the room to imitate the movie's sound effects. As he narrated the story, the room came alive with the roar of engines. The performance was a big hit with everyone except the guards, who eventually beat on the door and told us to quiet down.

In spite of our many innovative talents, there was one thing we couldn't create: females. But that didn't stop the guys in room two from having dancing lessons, in preparation for the good times that would surely come when we were released. They got through the basics, but it was hard to sustain the practice. One of my friends explained, "It was very awkward when it came my turn to play the lady's role." I guess there are a few things fighter pilots don't do very well.

⑦ LESSON: EXPLOIT CREATIVITY

"Necessity is the mother of invention," said Plato. We certainly found that to be true in the bare and deprived conditions of the POW camps. Innovation and creativity were essential for survival.

Innovation also is essential for survival in business. In a "2010 Global CEO Study" conducted by IBM, 60 percent of the 1,500+ CEOs interviewed said they believed creativity would be the most important attribute leaders must possess during the years ahead.[3] The study found that most CEOs don't believe their enterprises are adequately prepared for the twenty-first century business environment, which will be characterized by dynamically shifting global power centers, rapidly transforming industries, exponentially escalating amounts of information, more intrusive government regulation, and dramatically changing customer preferences.

The most successful leaders, the IBM study concludes, will highly value creativity and consistently pursue innovative ideas. They will readily welcome disruptive innovation, drop outdated approaches, take balanced risks, and be willing to totally reinvent themselves and their companies when necessary.

Forward-looking leaders have always done that. Andy Grove and Gordon Moore are a case in point. As early leaders of Intel Corporation, they asked themselves the question, "What would a new management do if we were kicked out and they were brought in?" The answer, they decided, was that smart leaders would get Intel out of the memory chip business. Armed with this new clarity, Andy and Gordon literally walked out of the company's offices, shut the door, and then reentered with a new perspective and a commitment to transition Intel into the microprocessor business. The rest is history.[4]

Organizations of all types—business, nonprofit, educational, and military—must innovate, but how do you manage it? Curtis Carlson, CEO of SRI International, made an observation that has become known as "Carlson's Law." He says, "In a world where so many people now have access to education and cheap tools of innovation, innovation that happens from the bottom up tends to be chaotic, but smart. Innovation that happens from the top down tends to be orderly, but dumb."[5] Visionary leaders stimulate progress by inviting, encouraging, and managing innovation from both the bottom and the top.

The Best Innovation Gets Results, Serves People, and Supports the Culture

As a leadership consultant, I have the opportunity to interact with a wide variety of leaders, most of whom are quite good.[6] But when it comes to innovation, Bob Pedersen, CEO of Goodwill Industries of North Central Wisconsin (Goodwill NCW), is unsurpassed. To begin with, Bob is an authentic leader who is comfortable with himself. He leads from the inside out and practices the leadership attributes outlined in this book. He and his outstanding team are not afraid to take risks and depart from conventional processes and mindsets, but they do not allow the organization to depart from its core value: "We put people first."[7]

The organization's supporting value, "We provide opportunities for the growth and development of people," provides the foundation of Goodwill's unique business model. This respected charity accepts donations of goods, sells them to the public, and uses the proceeds to help people who are struggling with disabilities, unemployment, and poverty. The organization itself provides jobs and job training to people who might otherwise be unemployed or unemployable.

This operational model is not unique—there are Goodwill facilities across the United States—but the commitment Bob and his team have made to inviting, encouraging, and managing innovation sets his organization apart. For example, a few years ago they diversified their offerings by opening the Harmony Café, a welcoming coffee house that celebrates the diversity of people (also a core value) in the community through arts, social interaction, and community involvement (another core value). This outreach provides jobs and revenues to expand other community support activities.

The organization's profits also fund personal development activities inside the organization. These programs are led and managed by Kris Hackbarth-Horn, whose title, COO People, underscores the importance of people in this "people business." For example, what most companies would call an employee handbook is an attractive publication called the *Gwizdom Handbook*. Another publication, the *Care-fronting Guidebook*, tells managers how to give positive and negative feedback in a way that balances good results and good relationships. All managers participate in the *Caring Leader Program*, which prescribes an intentional, structured approach for continuous growth of supervisors and managers.

If you are a highly results-oriented person, this creative, people-centric focus may sound soft. Many leaders fear that such a strong emphasis on people will undermine profitable performance, but just the opposite is true. At Goodwill NCW, it has boosted store revenues by more than 300 percent in the last ten years. Significant profits have been channeled into surrounding communities to help the disadvantaged become more independent. Bob and his excellent team have been reaping the benefits of innovation for several years. They didn't wait for the IBM study!

Leaders Must Exploit Creativity

Creativity exists in various forms. Some people are truly "out of the box" original thinkers. Their creative efforts are so innovative that revolutionary change results. Others are more concrete, and their innovation is more evolutionary in nature. They "connect the dots" and come up with ways to improve on current processes and on the original ideas of others. Both types of creativity are necessary and valuable.

As the leader, you do not need to be the most innovative person in your organization, nor do you need to birth every idea. However, you do need to cultivate an environment that fosters innovation and facilitates management of it. Here are some suggestions about how to do this:

Create a climate that values and encourages innovation. Remember in Chapter 7 how Ralph de la Vega, President and CEO, AT&T Mobility and Consumer Markets, challenged a task force to find and acquire disruptive technologies for the organization to develop and market? Innovative leaders come up with innovative ways to foster innovation.

Be intentional in your efforts to attract and develop creative people. Assess candidates for creativity, and hire based on your needs. Most organizations can only handle so many highly creative people. Keep in mind that highly imaginative people can become discouraged when they are not supported with the freedom and resources they need to innovate. On the other hand, leaders need a vetting process for new concepts, or else they'll be worn out by an endless stream of "crazy ideas." Properly supported and managed, a few highly creative people can make a significant contribution to a team.

Mine the minds of all your people. It pays to assume that all individuals are creatively talented in some way and to some degree. Even in room 3 with only fifty-five "military minds," we had more than enough creativity to launch a mini-university without a single book. One of a leader's main responsibilities is to identify the innovative talents of people and match them to the needs of the organization. People whose creativity is tapped tend to come alive with an energy and passion that is contagious.

 **Foot Stomper:** Think futuristically and innovate to stay competitive. Everyone has the capacity for innovative ideas; the leader's job is to draw them out. Harness the ideas of the creative folks, and allow them to pull you ahead of the competition.

⑦ Coaching: EXPLOIT CREATIVITY

Innovation and creativity are crucial in today's fast-changing world. Are you keeping up?

1. **What is your mindset about innovation?** Is it an integral part of your leadership philosophy? How do you manage innovation processes in your organization? Do you aggressively push for innovation and support creative people, or do you fear the risk of innovation and try to avoid it?

2. **Do you intentionally identify and exploit the talents of your most creative people?** Some assessment instruments, such as the *Leadership Behavior DNA™* Assessment mentioned earlier, will help you identify them. How do you evaluate their ideas and keep them motivated?[8]

3. **How do you draw out new ideas from those who are not naturally highly creative?** Is everyone thinking about ways to improve processes and improve efficiencies? Do you give a good hearing to the ideas of others?

Note: To download an expanded version of these coaching questions for writing your responses, visit LeadingWithHonor.com/Book.

---

[1] We never saw a normal flushable toilet in the camps. Some cells had a partially walled-off area for privacy. Two bricks were fastened to the concrete-slab floor for your feet, and there was a hole in the slab for the waste bucket.

[2] John Nasmyth, *2555 Days*. (New York, NY: Orion, 1991) 190-192.

[3] *IBM Global Study*, http://www-03.ibm.com/press/us/en/pressrelease/31670.wss (accessed Feb 26, 2011).

[4] As related by an Intel senior executive.

[5] Thomas L. Friedman. "Advice to China." *New York Times*, June 4, 2011.

[6] Enlightened and confident leaders want to grow and welcome help. Insecure leaders usually don't want anyone to hold up a mirror.

[7] For more on Goodwill Industries NCW and their values, see *Goodwill Industries*, http://www.goodwillncw.org/missionvision.htm (April 3, 2011).

[8] For help in learning more about your unique talents and leadership style with the *Leadership Behavior DNA™* Assessment, get started by taking the free *Leading with Honor Discovery Report* offered on page 234.

Chapter 13

TREASURE YOUR TRIALS AND CELEBRATE YOUR SUCCESSES

"Adversity has the effect of eliciting talents which, in prosperous circumstances, would have lain dormant."

Horace (65-68 B.C.)

When I first arrived in Hanoi in late November 1967, the approaching Christmas holidays were the furthest thing from my mind. So, when Fat in the Fire showed up at our peephole one morning with a smirk on his face and said, "Are you preparing for 'Creetmus,'?" I was speechless. We knew that the communists hated Christianity. Was this just a cruel joke, or were they planning some bizarre torture, perhaps even a crucifixion?

Seeing our dumbfounded expressions, Fat in the Fire repeated the question: "You know, are you ready to celebrate 'Creetmus,' you know sing Creetmus songs like '500 Miles'?" Sure enough, a couple of days before Christmas the camp radio speakers in our cell began playing "500 Miles" and songs by Joan Baez and Bob Dylan. There weren't many real Christmas songs, but the V did serve a special meal that included a salad, a slice of tough meat that was probably water buffalo, and a piece of hard candy.

The communists used almost every holiday—theirs and ours—for indoctrination and propaganda stunts. That first Christmas they broadcast a sermon telling us to repent and follow the communist way. In later years a few men were taken to Mass, but it turned out to be a propaganda photo op for the enemy. Our POWs made the best of it by communicating covertly with men from other compounds and other camps.

On occasional holidays the V would set out a banquet table of food for a selected group of POWs. When the guys dished the food onto their plates, the cameras started clicking—another staged photo-op. The photos were sent out to show the world how well we were eating. However, these false propaganda episodes did have one upside: for a day or two the pressure lifted and torture paused. As the members of the Strategic Air Command used to joke, our reward was no punishment.

We found that celebrating even little victories lifted our spirits, boosted our confidence, and strengthened our determination. It was always cause for celebration when a cellmate returned from solitary or from a torture session. When Ken came back after being kept awake in handcuffs and leg irons sitting on the stool for twenty-one days, we celebrated with him, even though hearing about his incredible ordeal pained our hearts and inflamed our anger.

When Jim Warner came back from six months of isolation in the "tank," we celebrated by listening to his new thousand-line epic poem and laughing with him about how an act of "divine intervention" had put one of the more onerous guards in his place. We called this guard "Oddjob" because he looked like a smaller version of the oriental bodyguard by that name in the James Bond movie *Goldfinger*.

As Oddjob was harassing Jim one day through the peephole of his cell, Jim suddenly pointed at him and let fly a string of curses and insults. It just so happened that a small thunderstorm had drifted over the camp, and just as Jim yelled and pointed his finger at Oddjob, a bolt of lightning flashed nearby with an accompanying ear-shattering clap of thunder. Oddjob's blood-curdling scream could be heard throughout the camp as he raced away. Thereafter, he would sneak by Jim's door like a whipped puppy, never again looking in.

Isolation in a communist prison is one of the loneliest experiences imaginable, so it was always cause for celebration when POWs were reunited with their cellmates after such punishment. The reunion conversations lasted for hours, often accompanied by hugs and tears. Air America pilot Ernie Brace, who spent five years in a cage in Laos and in the hinterlands of Vietnam, was so overwhelmed with emotion when he heard the voice of John McCain through the wall that he was unable to respond for several minutes. Every time he tried to say something, he broke down in tears. Walking together through these kinds of trials forged enduring bonds.

At Son Tay during the winter of 1970, Hanoi Hannah made an off-hand comment to the effect that if Neil Armstrong were to go to the DMZ [1], the craters would look very familiar to him. That statement about bomb craters was a subtle clue with an out-of-this-world message that could mean only one thing: the United States had landed a man on the moon. The V never gave us good news, so this unintended disclosure of a history-making event electrified us.

We immediately sent a message through the wall to get Alan Brudno (1st Lt USAF) "to the phone." Brudno had earned a degree in astronautics from MIT with the goal of becoming an astronaut, so we knew he was familiar with the details of the Apollo program. Using his blanket as a muffler, Alan yelled back through the wall to confirm what we had heard. Yes, our country had been to the moon, even ahead of schedule. This accomplishment was a huge boost to our morale at a time when we really needed a lift.

The next morning, when we stepped out in the compound and headed for the wash house, a crescent moon shown in the sky. Ken Fisher pointed to it and said, "Gentlemen, our flag is on that moon." The five of us came to attention, looked up to face the moon, and saluted. The guards had no idea what we were doing, but we did. We were celebrating.

Not long after we were moved to Camp Unity in late November of 1970, the V daily began giving us an orange and enough raw sugar for each person to have a couple of tablespoons. According to some of the optimists, this was a sign that the V were trying to fatten us and that meant we were going home soon. This habit of interpreting improvements in food quality or quantity as a sign that we were going home soon came to be known as "gastro-politics," a practice that never seemed to hold up. Unconvinced that we were nearing the end of the war, several of us wanted to do something special to commemorate our first holiday season together in a large group.

Richard "Dog" Brenneman (1st Lt, USAF) suggested that we make some orange wine to celebrate New Year's Eve. In this cell, we had three five-gallon water containers so Dog figured that our now unused one-liter ceramic water jugs would make perfect crocks for fermenting a mix of sugar and oranges into wine. About a third of us thought Dog's idea was worth trying and began saving the ingredients in our crocks. Soon we had enough to get the mash "cooking."

When the V conducted a search a few days before Christmas, we feared that the wine would be poured out or confiscated, especially when they ran across some real contraband—Dog's stash of materials that he was using to build a radio. Then the V flipped out and started the search anew. We were sure the wine would be gone.

Incredibly, they left the wine untouched. Unfortunately, Dog and his technical expert on the radio, the unflappable Mo Baker (Major, USAF), would miss the party. They got a roughing up and then spent the holidays in solitary in Heartbreak Hotel. On New Year's Eve, we brave souls who trusted Dog with our sugar and oranges shared our brew with the others and everyone ended up with about four ounces each.[2] We raised our tin cups and toasted the New Year, our country, our families, the MIAs, and our missing friends Dog and Mo. It was quite a celebration. And as it turned out, we would be there two more Christmas/New Year's holiday seasons.

Almost everyone celebrated his anniversary of shoot-down and capture in some small way, because it was the most significant event of our lives that we all shared in common. As Smitty Harris approached his seventh anniversary as a POW, a covert team in room 3 went to work planning a real extravaganza. Some of us knew his life story in intimate detail, so we had more than enough material to put on a first class "This is Your Life" roast. Tall and lanky Charley Green (Captain, USAF) had the perfect profile to play Miss Birdlegs Bradley, one of the more interesting characters in Smitty's past. The team did a great job of dressing Charley like a woman, complete with stuffed-sweater augmentation that would have rivaled the work of Hollywood's finest plastic surgeons.

The evening's celebration was a smashing success, but like most of our celebrations, it was bittersweet. Smitty's youngest son, Lyle, who had been born three months after his capture, was now almost seven. We could only imagine the heartaches that Smitty, his wife Louise, and their three children had endured. That evening, though, Smitty was smiling from ear to ear.

After dark on Mother's Day 1972, 208 of us were herded onto the back of tarp-covered trucks and driven north to a remote mountain camp only two miles from the Chinese border. There was no electricity in the camp. It was so primitive that we named it Dogpatch. The bombing had resumed in and around Hanoi, and if the capitol crumbled, we would be the V's bargaining chips in any negotiations. Toward December, when the Linebacker II operation began pounding Hanoi, we could see fear in the eyes of the V. Could the increased bombing be hastening the end of the war?

The answer came quickly. In early January 1973, our captors told us that progress had been made in Paris and that the war might soon be over. At dusk on January 19, we climbed into trucks and headed south, jostling along for nineteen hours. But the trip was very different from that first truck ride to Hanoi more than five years earlier. This time our spirits lifted with each bounce with the anticipation that we were moving closer to freedom. Even the guards seemed more relaxed. Late the next day, as we pulled into Hanoi, some of the trucks peeled off for the Hanoi Hilton. Our truck kept moving across town to the Plantation, a camp I had never seen, but knew about from many cellmates.

I was put in the Corn Crib with four Air Force comrades, under the leadership of Major Bob Barnett (USAF), who had been my SRO for a while up at Dogpatch. The rules were different now; we were allowed outside for most of each day to visit with all the men in the Plantation. When we realized that we had all been captured in the same time frame (late 1967 through early 1968), we were greatly encouraged. This turned out to be an accurate sign that they were preparing to release us in order of capture, as our camp policy had prescribed.

A few days later we were directed to assemble in the yard. Through an interpreter, the camp commander told us that an agreement had been signed in Paris ending the war, and that we would go home in several groups over a two-month period in concert with the final withdrawal of the U.S. from South Vietnam. There were no cheers or any display of emotion whatsoever. We were not going to celebrate, only to have our hopes dashed. Besides that, we were concerned they might use our celebration as a photo-op for a propaganda piece.

We were each given a copy of the protocol to the agreement regarding the release of POWs. Some of the men stood around in groups reading it; others took it back to their rooms. It was an official document clarifying the agreement and our impending release. This was the best sign yet that the day we had been hoping and praying for was near.

That evening we gathered out in the yard. It was a mellow time. Some groups were walking and talking with cellmates from the old days. Others were just hanging out. After awhile, we heard music and saw that a group had gathered around Bill Butler, who had somehow convinced the V to lend him a guitar. Before long we had a songfest going. The atmosphere was relaxed, as if we were sitting around a campfire while on vacation at the beach. Gradually the heavy burden of worry that our minds had carried for so long began to slip away.

The V locked us in at 10:00 p.m. each evening, but the anticipation made it difficult to sleep. We were like little children waiting for the opening of presents on Christmas Day. Sensing that we needed something to pass the time, the V opened the storehouse of books that our families had sent over the years, and handed out one book to each room. We read them aloud so we could all enjoy them together. In the days leading up to our release we finished several good ones, including *Hawaii* by James Michener, *Kabloona* by Gontran de Poncins, and, best of all, *Man's Search for Meaning* by Victor Frankl.

It was an amazing experience sitting in a POW camp reading Frankl's monumental book about surviving the Holocaust. Although his trials were much more severe than ours were, we all felt a special kinship with him. I could never have imagined that within sixty days I would be listening to Frankl speak at the University of Georgia.[3]

During the years that Ken Fisher, Denver Key, Ted Stier, Jim Warner and I lived together, one of us would regularly say to another, "Ken, is this the day?" or, "Jim, is this the day?" The answer would always be, "No, I'm sorry but today is not the day." On the morning of March 14, 1973, we walked across the camp to a storeroom and picked up our departure clothing. As we did, Jim looked across at me and said, "Leon, this is the day."

⑦ LESSON: TREASURE YOUR TRIALS AND CELEBRATE YOUR SUCCESSES

Character cannot be developed in ease and quiet.
Only through experience of trial and suffering
can the soul be strengthened, ambition inspired,
and success achieved.

Helen Keller

Character is perfected in hardship; talents are refined in the crucible of trials. As Victor Frankl put it, "When we are no longer able to change a situation, we are challenged to change ourselves." The painful struggles we would never choose often offer the greatest opportunity for personal growth, and personal growth is the only path to genuine leadership development. In fact, leadership coaching guru Marshall Goldsmith titled his best selling book *What Got You Here Won't Get You There*. In the camps as we began to exercise to build our strength, we put it even more bluntly: "Pain purifies."

Learn from the Crucibles

Like it or not, we tend to learn the most about ourselves in our struggles. Such self-awareness is the prerequisite for all personal development. I'm not suggesting that we need to enjoy trials, but as individuals and leaders we do need to value them. In his foreword to Bill George's best selling book *True North*, Warren Bennis says, "One of the revelations of *True North* is how critical these leaders' personal stories are in shaping their leadership. Time after time, those interviewed describe a turning point in their lives—a crucible, I call it—that transformed them into the leaders they are today."[4]

Leadership guru Dr. Bob Thomas, executive director of the Institute of High Performance at Accenture, also an associate of Warren Bennis, has pointed out the benefits of trials for developing leaders. I met Bob at an Air Force symposium in San Antonio a few months after beginning this book, and I was naturally attracted to his presentation based on his book *Crucibles of Leadership*. It was thrilling to hear him say that "great leaders become great by finding meaning in adversity—in traumatic and unplanned crucible experiences—and then transforming those experiences into improved performance." His research strongly supports my contention that crucibles such as POW camps develop leadership qualities. Likewise, the trials in your life can burn away the dross and make you a better person and a better leader.

Clearly, the best leadership development comes from our own experiences. However, as I said in the Introduction, I believe we can also learn indirectly from the stories of others, especially when we have an emotional connection with them. When you are facing a situation that requires courage and sacrifice, I hope you will be inspired by someone you read about in this book. Take courage from those who leaned into the pain and made conscious decisions to live and lead with honor.

Because wisdom and maturity are forged in trials, I would think twice before hiring someone for an executive leadership role who has not been humbled through significant struggles. Leaders devoid of crucible experiences are likely to be overly confident about their ideas, less sensitive to those of others, and surprisingly more susceptible to fears. Leaders motivated by fears and selfishness tend to make choices and cultivate attitudes that undermine the growth of the organization and its people.

I realize that this discussion about treasuring trials may seem like a "chicken and egg" scenario. After all, which comes first: the character or the trial? We've talked about how trials develop character and talents, but isn't character necessary in order to successfully survive trials? The answer, of course, is that decent leaders have a basic foundation of character to begin with and as character is refined by trials, it becomes even stronger. When we adopt a long-term perspective, we will increasingly learn to treasure our trials for the character they develop in us.

Celebrate Your Successes

Celebrations have been important since the beginning of time. Every culture has feasts and holidays to commemorate important events and achievements. Each member of the team that wins the Super Bowl receives a big ring, a big paycheck, a trip to the White House, and accolades that go on for years. Modern Olympic victors receive their medals standing on a podium before a worldwide TV audience.

However, isn't it true that most of us celebrate too little? Although our celebrations in the POW camps had to be simple and subdued, they were powerful boosts to our morale, our teamwork, and our ongoing ability to achieve the mission. Too often people celebrate only the big successes and victories, and they forget that celebrating modest victories in the day-to-day battles of work and life is important too, especially in times of trial. Over the years as POWs, we did not have "the big day" to celebrate, so we focused more on the small events. Likewise, I've noticed that some of the most successful companies, which are also often the best places to work, have regular celebrations instead of waiting for some "big event."

One of my clients, Shaun Callahan, President and CEO of Georgia Fluid System Technologies (a Swagelok® distributor), is one of the most creative leaders I've seen when it comes to orchestrating meaningful celebrations.[5] Typically, he ties them to specific quarterly and yearly milestones, which are aligned with corporate goals and clearly delineated in his Gazelle's system of tracking.[6]

Each year he relates the unit's goals and rewards to a theme that is highly visible to everyone. For example, one year the theme was "Sailing Away," and team members filled in the portholes on a ship poster as goals were achieved. At the end of a very successful year, the entire office celebrated by taking a four-day cruise, complete with luau shirts and a banquet.

The following year the theme was "Climbing Higher," which encouraged employees to reach the pinnacle of another mountain each quarter. At the end of the year, the team headed west for a three-day celebration at Lake Tahoe. The energy stayed high throughout the year, because Shaun and his team consistently celebrated "above and beyond" performances in weekly meetings.

Celebrations validate our deep human need for confirmation of purpose and affirmation of accomplishments. People who feel valued tend to be more energetic, enthusiastic, proud, and confident. These emotions produce the kind of positive energy that drives results and facilitates fulfillment. That's why companies that emphasize celebrations are typically good places to work.

Wal-Mart founder, Sam Walton, expressed his thoughts on the subject saying, "Celebrate your success and find humor in your failures. Don't take yourself so seriously. Loosen up and everyone around you will loosen up. Have fun and always show enthusiasm. When all else fails, put on a costume and sing a silly song."[7]

Unfortunately, many leaders shy away from celebrating victories and successes. Some fear that celebrating sets the bar too high. What if a particular achievement is never duplicated? If successes are celebrated, won't failures be harder to ignore? Obviously, this view springs from a negative attitude founded in fear. And as we have discussed so often in this book, fear can be a powerful hindrance to good leadership behaviors and habits. Secure leaders know perfection is not realistic, and that downturns happen to the best. They believe they can lead through the storms as well as the calm waters.

But there's an even more common objection to celebrations. Some leaders feel that if team members are allowed to have fun, they will relax and begin to rest on their laurels. Indeed, that can happen in some cases. Secure leaders understand that most people want to do a good job; they are interested in achieving, not goofing off.

We all need varying quantities of fun in our lives. Regardless of where your natural fun meter pegs, you will likely need to ramp it up for managing the cohort of Generation Y. According to Tim Elmore, president of Growing Leaders and author of the new book *Generation iY*, "They believe work and fun can be combined; they don't want to separate the two. In fact, they may stop working midday to have fun and work again at midnight. It's a continuum."[8] If you are a boomer managing this new generation, don't let this be a cause for fear. Look for the treasure in your trials with Generation Y. Remember, most people want to achieve and are much more productive when they have positive emotions—the kind that come from frequent celebrations of small victories.

Foot Stomper: Effective leadership is forged in the crucible of struggles and fueled by the celebration of accomplishment. To promote teamwork and achieve success, treasure your trials and celebrate your victories.

⑦ Coaching: TREASURE YOUR TRIALS AND CELEBRATE YOUR SUCCESSES

The treasures that are often hidden in our suffering and trials can provide greater clarity about what is really true about ourselves and about life in general.

1. **What treasures have you discovered in your trials?** Truths about yourself? Truths about life? Wisdom about leadership? Insights about your leadership?

2. **How have these treasures helped you as a leader?** How do you lead differently as a result of what you learned in your crucibles? Looking forward, will your insights about trials be different? If so, how?

3. **What is your perspective on celebrating?** Is your view more positive or negative? What fears do you have about celebrating? Are you too quick to celebrate?

4. **What changes would you like to make in your attitude and behaviors related to celebrations?** Would it help for you to be more intentional and use more planning in your approach to celebrating?

Note: To download an expanded version of these coaching questions for writing your responses, visit LeadingWithHonor.com/Book.

---

[1] DMZ is the acronym used for Demilitarized Zones, as there still exists between North and South Korea.

[2] Our brew tasted more like a mild brandy than wine.

[3] My high school and college friend, Dr. John B. Hardman, arranged with host Dr. Edith Weisskoph-Joelson, University of Georgia, Department of Psychology, for me to meet with Victor Frankl following his presentation.

[4] Bill George and Peter Sims, *True North: Discover Your Authentic Leadership*. (San Francisco, CA: Jossey-Bass, 2007) xiv.

[5] Georgia Fluid Systems Technologies, based in Alpharetta, GA, represents Swagelok® in Georgia and northern Florida with high tech products for steam producers, such as the paper and nuclear power industries.

[6] Based on Verne Harnish, *Mastering the Rockefeller Habits*. (New York, NY: Select-

Books, Inc., 2002). See *Classic One Page Worksheet*, http://www.gazelles.com/one-page_ strategic_plan_template.html.

[7] *Sam Walton Quotes and Sayings*, www.searchquote.com (accessed June 9,2011).

[8] Tim Elmore, comment on "8 Terms to Understand Generation Y," Tim Elmore on Leading the Next Generation, Growing Leaders, Comment posted December 1, 2010. http:// blog.growingleaders.com/generation-iy/8-terms-to-understand-generation-y/ (accessed April 10, 2011).

Chapter 14

FREE THE CAPTIVES

★

*"Caged birds accept each other
but flight is what they long for."*

Tennessee Williams, *Camino Real*

Early on our final day of captivity, the V issued each of us a pair of dark blue cotton slacks, a long-sleeve blue shirt, a gray windbreaker, a small gym bag, and a pair of shoes. We didn't waste any time getting dressed. For the first time in more than five years we would be wearing something other than black or maroon striped pajamas. My feet had become so accustomed to rubber tire treads held on by a strap across the toe that I wondered if I would have trouble putting on real shoes. It was not a problem.

A little before noon we loaded onto camouflage-colored buses, and our motorcade headed for Gia Lam Airport. It was a strange feeling to be outside the prison walls without blindfolds, handcuffs, and leg irons. We rode like normal people taking in the city and gazing back at the curious Vietnamese onlookers. After a short ride, we pulled into a park near the airport, and they handed us a box lunch and a bottle of Vietnamese beer. Our excitement began to rise, but we were still calm— steady on course.

After lunch, the buses took us to the airport, where we unloaded and formed up on the tarmac in groups based on date of capture. John McCain was in the first row of our group, and I was three rows behind him.

Yes, this was the day—the long-awaited day—and we were functioning as if it was just another day at work. To be honest, I was more curious than excited. I had grown to be so cautious that my emotions were as flat as a table. After five years, four months, and two weeks—

1,955 days of captivity—I was going to walk through this exercise and see what happened.

March 14, 1973, Release - Hanoi Gia Lam Airport, McCain front row, Lee Ellis and Ken Fisher on the fourth row.

As our names were called, we stepped forward and saluted the senior U.S. Air Force officer who was receiving us. We were then escorted to three waiting C-141s, a bird ever after to be known as the Hanoi Taxi. When all were loaded, the walk-on tailgates were closed and the windowless aircraft, which felt inside somewhat like a cave, began taxiing out. The lack of visibility brought to mind a trip I had taken less than a year earlier, when we were transported under a tarp in the back of a truck from Hanoi north to Dogpatch. On today's journey, though, there would be no blindfolds, handcuffs, guards, or bone-jarring bounces.

The revving of the C-141's four big engines caused my heart to race. Pilots love the feeling of power during the run-up and takeoff; this time it was almost surreal. As the brakes released and our Hanoi Taxi accelerated smoothly down the runway, we held our breath waiting…waiting…waiting. Finally, the wheels broke ground—we were airborne! A bedlam of cheers, yells, whistles, and foot stomps erupted in the cabin.

Our destination was the big hospital at Clark Air Base in the Philippines. As the primary Air Force staging base in both the Korean and Vietnam wars, it was a familiar place to most of us. A few minutes after takeoff, the aircraft commander came on the intercom: "Gentlemen, we are 'feet wet' and over international waters." A roar went up; the captives indeed were free.

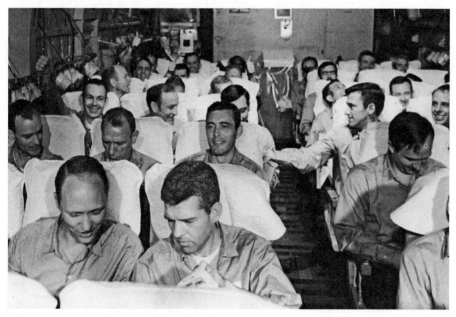

Flying home on the Hanoi Taxi. In this picture, Lee is in the 5th row, right side.

On the flight to Clark AB, we smoked cigars, circulated, shook hands, looked at the latest magazines, and visited the cockpit, where I was taken aback to see that the aircraft commander was a captain about my age, still under thirty. We also took turns hugging the three nurses on board. Other than a couple of Vietnamese kitchen coolies, we had not seen a female in all those years.

As the Hanoi Taxi rolled into the VIP parking space at Clark, we were surprised to see a large crowd waiting with welcome signs and banners. As we deplaned, the cheers and tears of the crowd warmed our hearts and calmed our anxieties about our reentry into a radically altered world.[1] It was a shock to be treated like returning heroes. We did not see ourselves as heroic; we simply had done our duty.

We went straight to the hospital, checked into our rooms, traded the Vietnamese travel clothes for hospital attire, and headed to the cafeteria for the thing we had most thought and talked about during captivity: food! It was afternoon, but the time of day didn't affect our menu choices. I had eggs (fried and scrambled), sausage, bacon, grits, hash browns, fruit, pancakes, and the long-awaited glass of cold orange juice. Then I returned for a steak and some ice cream, followed by more ice cream with apple pie. My friend Leroy Stutz (Captain, USAF), who had been released ten days earlier with a group of men shot down in 1966, had set the record. This farm boy from Kansas and former football player at the Air Force Academy, ate a dozen eggs with all the trimmings and then went back and got a dozen more followed by a couple of steaks and then several desserts.

After our meal, we started working the phones to call home. As a single guy, my call was to my parents, who were waiting at our farmhouse with my brother and his family. It was wonderful to hear their voices again and to know that all was well. These calls were a dream come true for most of us, but not for all. Some men learned that their wives had moved on or wanted a divorce; a few found out for the first time that a parent had passed away.

We spent two days at Clark getting a brief physical, dental check, haircut, and new uniforms for the journey home. Putting on that blue service uniform was an emotional experience. It represented my career, the commitment I had made, and the sacrifices that had come with it. I was proud to wear it again; it had been a privilege to serve my country in difficult times and in the presence of true heroes. We were a band of brothers. We had accomplished our mission, and we had returned with honor.

Those of us returning to the southeastern United States came back together, stopping only once to refuel in Hawaii. It was the middle of the night when we arrived at Hickam Air Force Base near Honolulu, but a large crowd was waiting to welcome us. Major General "Boots" Blesse, a Korean War ace and one of my commanders in Vietnam, was there to greet our flight. He and I had flown several combat missions together, and it was good to see him again.

After a short visit, we were back in the air for a nonstop flight to Montgomery, Alabama. It was hard to believe that I'd soon be back in the sunny South, the land of pines, peaches, pretty girls, and grits. We Air Force guys would undergo a few days of detailed medical exams and intelligence debriefings at the Air Force Regional Hospital at Maxwell AFB. John McCain and the Navy guys would board another aircraft and head on down to Jacksonville, where they would be reunited with their families and check into the regional hospital.

This C-141 was configured for a med-evac flight, so I crawled into a bunk and began to reflect on what was happening. After nearly six years in captivity, POW life had become the norm. How well would I adapt to a world where a myriad of changes had occurred and a multitude of opportunities waited? Even simple activities, like sitting in a chair, having a hot shower, or drinking beverages with ice would require an adjustment. How out of step would I be, and how would others experience me? The only thing I knew for sure was that I would never be quite the same. Yes, I was the same person—adventurous, confident, outgoing, and blunt—but I had changed in profound ways, mostly for the better. While pondering these thoughts, I sank into a deep sleep.

About an hour out, we were awakened so we could freshen up and prepare for arrival. This was the day I had been waiting for. I had always believed it would come, but now that it had arrived, I wondered what it would be like. I straightened my tie and put on my uniform jacket. At the last minute I decided to wear the lei I had been given at our stopover in Hawaii. The cockpit reported that the weather on the ground was clear and crisp, a perfect March day.

We landed, taxied in, and deplaned one at a time. When they

announced my name, I walked down the steps, saluted the dignitaries, and stepped over to the staff car where my mom and dad waited with open arms—a terrific moment! Our escort officer drove us to the officer's quarters where my brother Robert, his wife Pat, and their son Bob were waiting for our joyful reunion. It was St. Patrick's Day, and I love green; but in pilot speak, it was all "blue skies." The dark clouds of POW life truly had passed, and the light of freedom was brightly shining. We celebrated throughout the rest of the day and long into the night.

Deplaning at Maxwell AFB, Montgomery, AL, March 17, 1973

Over two delightful days we caught up on what had happened to each of us during the past five and a half years. For the first time I saw my three-year-old nephew, Bob, and I also met Ken Fisher's lovely wife, Maggie. When he was captured, they had been married only two and a half years. It was strange to realize that Ken and I had lived together more than twice that long. When Ken had left the States, his little girl, Susan, was ten months old; now she was a grown-up six.

After our families headed home, we "returnees" kept our quarters and signed into the hospital to begin physical checkups. The majority of us were in decent health. I had lost several fillings due to rocks in the rice, and like the rest of the guys, I needed de-worming. The guys who had suffered serious bone damage on ejection and capture had the most problems; some would need significant surgeries to correct years of neglect.

During the next month we would spend many hours with the intelligence debriefers telling our stories in minute detail. The immediate objective was to gather any information we might have about non-returning POWs and MIAs. As far as I knew, no one was aware of any living POW left behind.

As soon as the first round of checks and intel debriefs was completed, I flew to Atlanta where my family picked me up. As our car approached our home, I noticed yellow ribbons on trees and fences along the side of the highway. With the war ending, the song "Tie A Yellow Ribbon ('Round The Old Oak Tree)" by Tony Orlando and Dawn sold more than three million copies in a matter of weeks and was number one on the charts for four weeks that spring. In our wildest dreams back in the camps, we never could have imagined how much of the nation's attention and concern had been focused on us. We owed a tremendous debt to the families, friends, and citizens who had worked so devotedly to raise awareness of our plight.

When we reached the city limits of Commerce, Georgia, the general manager of the local GMC dealership, Milton Nix, was waiting in a Cadillac convertible. Being driven down the main street of my hometown to the cheers of hundreds of citizens was an overwhelming experience. In retrospect, I regret that my parents, my brother, Robert, and his wife, Pat, were not in that convertible with me. Their years of work and sacrifice on my behalf made them the real heroes in my eyes.

It's unfortunate that another group of real heroes—our Vietnam veterans who made tremendous sacrifices for our country—were not welcomed home as were the POWs. The majority of our vets never received a word of thanks, and many were treated with disdain, even

Greeting faithful supporters in Commerce, GA
Photo © Ron Sherman

hostility. It did not seem fair that we were honored and they were not.

A few weeks later, those of us who had lived at Son Tay, along with the Son Tay raiders who had attempted to free us, were flown by Ross Perot to San Francisco for a reunion party. After a parade in streetcars and a cruise in the harbor, we were treated to a huge banquet at the Fairmont Hotel with entertainment by numerous celebrities, including Red Skelton and the Andrews Sisters. John Wayne and Clint Eastwood were there to pay homage to the "real" tough guys. At dinner, Duke, with tears in his eyes, turned to raid leader and legendary special operations commander Colonel Arthur "Bull" Simons and said, "Colonel, you are in real life the role I only play in the movies."[2]

The celebrations seemed to go on and on. Ross Perot, with the support of civic leaders and several Texas corporations, invited five hundred of us, along with our spouses or guests, to Dallas for a Texas-size celebration. This gigantic affair, dubbed *Dallas Salutes*, was the first time all Vietnam POWs had been together. What a privilege it was to meet men I had known about for years but had never seen. On Saturday afternoon, we sat on the field at the Cotton Bowl as Bob Hope hosted a special tribute to us before 70,000 fans. When Tony Orlando and Dawn finished singing their hit song "Tie A Yellow Ribbon," all in attendance were on their feet cheering.

We were invited to the White House in May for what turned out to be the largest party ever held on the premises. The celebrities who entertained us sat at our tables. Sammy Davis Jr. was seated between my mom and me and was a gracious and entertaining host. Bob Hope again emceed and kept us laughing all night. At the close of this magnificent evening, the elderly Irving Berlin stepped onto the stage, spoke a few words of kindness, and then led us in "God Bless America;" there wasn't a dry eye in the place. Truly, the "faith you can never afford to lose" had become reality.

Like most of the POWs, I had decided to continue my career in the service. The Air Force had instituted a plan called Operation Homecoming to requalify returning pilots, so on August 7, 1973, under the watchful eye of my instructor pilot, I launched a T-38 out of Randolph AFB in San Antonio. As we cleared the end of the runway, I rotated the "white rocket" into a max climb, pressed the mic button and the made the call to the tower, "Freedom 34, airborne." This captive was really free; I had slipped the surly bonds of earth once more.

⑦ LESSON: FREE THE CAPTIVES

Captivity was not without its benefits. One of them was the opportunity afforded for reflection. At times I felt as if I was on a silent retreat. In these quiet moments, I realized that my physical body wasn't the only thing imprisoned. My mind also needed to be set free from bondage to unhelpful perceptions, erroneous opinions, and self-limiting fears.

This awareness motivated me to fight new battles for my own freedom, and it allowed me to become more sensitive to the kinds of shackles that inhibit others. As a leadership consultant, I've noticed that even good leaders typically have not yet arrived in their journey to freedom and wholeness. Most will need to address one or more of these three issues to free themselves and in turn free others: (1) avoid bitterness, (2) connect with their emotions, and (3) do the right thing in spite of the difficulty.

Avoid Bitterness

Since my release, people have often said to me, "I can't believe you're not bitter." That's an understandable question, considering that I "lost" more than five prime years of my life. However, I don't feel bitter. During our last two years of captivity, when the V adopted more of a "live and let live" policy, we had time to think about our feelings and about what our attitudes would be after repatriation. Most of us concluded that bitterness would serve no good purpose, but would instead undermine our happiness and steal our freedom. Bitterness is about looking back with anger and regrets. "Victims" who focus on their losses and blame others for their misfortunes make poor leaders.

I also harbor no bitterness toward those who objected to the war. In the camps we were proud to defend the rights of the protesters back home, even when we believed their actions prolonged the war and consequently our term of imprisonment. My cellmates and I regularly told the communists that freedom of speech was one thing that made our way of life great and theirs unacceptable.

Life is full of opportunities to become bitter; "injustice" is everywhere. One person may feel cheated when he is passed over for a promotion that goes to a "less competent" colleague. Another may become bitter when she loses her job or has a career fall apart for no apparent reason. Still another may indulge in self-pity when he loses his life's savings due to poor advice or a scam. When parents lose a child, or have a child born with a severe disability, bitterness knocks at the door of their hearts wanting to come in. And it's easy for those who suffer the injustice and humiliation of discrimination to feel like victims. There are many reasons that seem to justify bitterness, but bitterness is always a losing proposition.

As a leader and coach, I try to help others understand that bitterness poisons the heart and imprisons the spirit. The consequences can be far worse than physical confinement. If you detect bitterness in yourself or others, launch a mission to free the captives. The first step for me was to look ahead to what is possible, rather than stew over being a victim. The antidote to bitterness is forgiveness. Forgiveness is usually grounded in love—and it starts with love for yourself. I refused to be bitter because I cared too much about myself to let someone or some situation that I could not control, ruin my life. When you really love yourself, you are more free to forgive and even love those who have hurt you.

Forgiveness also comes more easily when you realize, as we pointed out in Chapter 13, that the most difficult trials can produce the greatest growth. In a very real sense, the years I spent in captivity in Vietnam were not "lost" or "wasted" at all; I reap some benefit from them almost every day. I certainly wouldn't choose to go back into captivity, but I appreciate the treasure that I've mined from those trials.

Connect with Your Emotions

Some of the toughest leaders I've known avoid emotions like the plague, except for anger, which they deem okay when it's theirs. Except in combat, shutting down your emotions is a mistake. Emotions can be a leader's greatest asset for positively influencing others.

Gallup Research shows that organizations where leaders emotionally engage with employees and customers realize significant financial returns. Specifically, the data revealed that customers who have a strong emotional connection to the organization deliver an average of 23 percent more than the average customer in terms of share-of-wallet, profitability, revenue, and relationship growth. In stark contrast, Gallup also found that actively disengaged customers—those whose emotional connection to an organization is weak or absent—represent a 13 percent *discount*.[3]

Emotional awareness is crucial for success on an individual level too. A few years ago I was brought in to coach a high-level superstar in a Fortune 500 company. He was brilliant and likeable, but in meetings he attempted to demonstrate his competence in an overly passionate, sometimes domineering, manner. During our second session I looked him in the eye and said, "Sam, I want to ask you a question. Who are you trying to impress?"

For a moment he was dumbstruck, as if I had hit him in the head with a hammer. After a long pause, he looked at me in astonishment and said, "My father, and he died two years ago." I reminded him that he was a highly paid, highly respected professional, and most likely his father would be proud of him. Even if that weren't true, he did not need to let self-doubts rule his life. Upon my recommendation, he entered into counseling and continued his growth.

Connecting with emotions has been one of my biggest personal struggles. As a POW, I worked to suppress my feelings to avoid the painful oscillations from highs to lows. That wasn't difficult for me to do. By personality, I tend to avoid most emotions except anger, which sometimes can be helpful for bringing about change and getting work done. When my second roommate of the war was shot down and lost, it hurt so much that I decided to shut down all sad emotions. In war, mourning every loss can land you in a bottomless pit of paralyzing despair and ineffectiveness. This decision served me well in the POW camps, but when I came home it started to cause problems, especially two years later when I met and married Mary. How can a husband whose emotions are encased in concrete connect at a heart level with his wife and children?

About fifteen years ago, I saw the magnitude of the problem. With this new awareness, I began to fight for a different kind of freedom in order to be able to give my family the unconditional love they needed. It's an ongoing process, but Mary will tell you that many of the fetters have fallen away. Seeing how my emotional freedom has given my family new freedom has been a strong incentive for me to lean into the pain.

PTSD (Post Traumatic Stress Disorder) increasingly is recognized as a serious problem among combat veterans.[4] But many executives in civilian life also suffer from the debilitating effects of insecurities and fears due to past hurts and traumas. Although the manifestations may be less severe than for combat veterans, the effects can be career derailing. If you suspect that mental or emotional bondages are holding you back, I encourage you to seek help, lean into the pain, and realize the rewards of an intentional commitment to growth.

Do the Right Thing

The strongest commitment I made coming home was to always try to do what is right. That's seldom easy, and sometimes I've fallen short, mostly due to impatience, anger, and fear. Now that I've become more aware of my emotions, I try to pause and determine what is driving them, so I can better understand how they are connected to my deepest desires and needs. Then I decide what actions would best allow me to live and lead in a way that honors God, my family, and my country.

Sometimes I catch myself struggling to clarify what is the right thing to do. This usually happens when I have strong emotions about one direction or the right choice requires doing something uncomfortable or unnatural. In these cases, I coach myself to "lean into the pain." When I have trouble being objective about what is the right thing to do, I reach out to my support team for counsel. If the issues are especially complex, I seek the assistance of a professional coach.

I think others notice my commitment to do the right thing and that helps me as a leader and coach. Not long ago one of my clients called me to ask my advice about whether she should buy a certain business to supplement the substantial income she earned from her regular job. This up-and-coming young executive had done extensive research, and she was very excited about the revenue potential of "moonlighting."

As a coach, it would have been inappropriate for me to tell her what to do, so I asked her a few questions about her motivation and her relationship with her current manager. "I want to buy this business so I can make more money," she answered, "and I don't plan to tell my manager right now." When I asked how she thought her manager would view her moonlighting idea, she replied, "He probably would not be happy if he found out." After I asked a few more questions to help her fully understand both her motives and the possible outcomes of her actions, she thanked me and said goodbye.

The next day this client called to say that she had decided to drop the idea, because her planned course of action did not meet the smell test of doing the right thing. As a footnote, within a short time she got a significant promotion and salary increase at her regular job. Meanwhile, the economy turned sour, and the business she had considered buying dried up.

Having had similar entrepreneurial urges as I approached retirement from the Air Force, I can understand this young lady's passion for owning her own business. I was very impressed with her willingness to process the idea in light of her personal commitment to lead honorably. Since then, it's become evident that her managers appreciate both her initiative and her character. I think she has a very bright future.

Foot Stomper: Authentic leaders proactively identify the shackles that hold them back and lean into the pain to break free and grow. As you gain your own freedom, begin helping others to do the same. Start by avoiding bitterness, connecting with your emotions, and doing the right thing even when it's difficult.

⑦ Coaching: FREE THE CAPTIVES

Most leaders do not think of themselves as captives, but everyone has some areas that are holding them back from being all they can be— habits and behaviors that just aren't working. Awareness is the starting point for gaining full freedom to grow in leading with honor. Likewise, once you recognize your own need for freedom, you will be able to help others break free also.

1. **Is it possible that past disappointments have created a hint of bitterness in your heart toward someone or some group?** Begin monitoring your strongest emotions for indications of bitterness. If it is present, what can you do about it? How can you help others who might be dealing with bitterness?

2. **How well are you connecting with your emotions?** If you are like many leaders, you may be having difficulty even recognizing them, let alone connecting with them. Refer to the emotions chart in Appendix E and find your most frequently recurring emotions. Are they positive or negative? How can you manage your emotions to be more effective as a leader? What are you doing to help others connect with their emotions?

3. **Reflect on a time when you rationalized and avoided doing what you knew was the right thing to do.** What can you learn from that experience? How are you helping others learn the value of doing what is right, even when it does not feel right?

Note: To download an expanded version of these coaching questions for writing your responses, visit LeadingWithHonor.com/Book.

---

[1] What we didn't know then but would soon learn was that most of our fellow veterans received no such honors. In fact they were generally dishonored for their service, which only added to the pain of war they brought back with them.

[2] For the exciting details of this raid, read *The Raid: The Son Tay Rescue Mission*, by Ben Schemmer.

[3] Gallup Consulting. "The Next Discipline: Applying Behavioral Economics to Drive Growth and Profitability." http://www.gallup.com/consulting/122906/next-discipline.aspx (2009)

[4] Many years after the war, several POW friends and I have recognized that we had some symptoms of PTSD. For me it was hyper-vigilance, recurring thoughts of having to fight bad guys, excessive need to be in control, and unnecessary anger. That awareness has been very helpful in gaining more freedom.

EPILOGUE

The ordeal was finally over. How wonderful it was to return home to the love of family and friends! Having lost my liberty for five and a half years, I now cherished it to the fullest.

The practical challenges of adjusting to freedom were mainly keeping up with my "stuff" and having to make so many decisions each day. In the camps we could carry all our possessions in our hands, which we did whenever we moved. Back home and surrounded by so many possessions, I had difficulty just keeping up with my car keys. And, with so many choices each day, even a trip to the grocery store could be exhausting.

But overall, adjusting was not a problem. It was natural and energizing to return to freedom and resume my life and career.

Character Breeds Success

There's a popular notion, perhaps promoted by the media, that most Vietnam veterans are societal failures. But studies reveal just the opposite. In fact, veterans have outperformed their peers by virtually every measure of success.[1] The discipline, maturity, and sense of responsibility gained from the military experience equipped them for significant accomplishments.

From our POW group came sixteen generals, six admirals, two U.S. ambassadors, two college presidents, two U.S. senators, one U.S. representative, and several state legislators. At least three men returned to medical school and became doctors; quite a few became attorneys; several became CEOs of corporations; and seven became attachés in U.S. Embassies abroad.

You've already read about the post-war successes of several individuals. I'll take a moment here to tell you about the achievements of a few more.

In retirement, VADM Jim Stockdale became president of The Citadel and the vice-presidential candidate on the ticket with Ross Perot. As a fellow at the Hoover Institution at Stanford University, he was a close colleague of Jim Collins, the best-selling leadership author who popularized the Stockdale Paradox mentioned earlier.

Brig Gen Robbie Risner commanded an air division when he returned. After retiring from the service, he headed the Texas War on Drugs for a number of years.

After repatriation, RADM Jeremiah Denton became superintendent of the Armed Forces Staff College. After retirement, he was elected a U.S. Senator from Alabama. Today he heads the Admiral Jeremiah Denton Foundation, which promotes fundamental American values and provides global humanitarian aid.

Col Ken Fisher had a distinguished flying career after Vietnam and served on the faculty at the Air War College. When he retired from the service, he became a successful financial planner.

In civilian life, Gen Chuck Boyd has served as strategy consultant to the Speaker of the U.S. House of Representatives, executive director of the U.S. Commission on National Security for the 21st Century, and senior vice president of the Council on Foreign Relations. From 2002 until 2009, he was president and CEO of Business Executives for National Security (BENS).

Brig Gen Jon Reynolds earned a PhD in history, taught at the Air Force Academy, and served on the Pentagon staff. Jon was selected as the first Air Attaché (later Defense Attaché) to Communist China. He was probably the only one from our language klatch in Unity room 3 to learn Mandarin Chinese.

Jim Warner separated from the Marine Corps upon his return and enrolled at the University of Michigan, where he earned his BA and JD degrees. He served as a corporate attorney, and later became a domestic policy advisor in the Reagan Administration. For the last twenty years of his career he served as an attorney advising not-for-profits in Washington, DC.

CAPT Denver Key, USN, our talented math and calculus instructor in room 3, taught at the Naval Academy for several years. In retirement, he continues to teach at a local community college.

Bill Butler, our lead French professor and the creative genius who taught us music, became a successful veterinarian.

The proficiency that Col Jay Jayroe gained in our Spanish language classes in room 3 helped him to become an Air Attaché to Venezuela. In retirement, he promoted the merits of the F-16 aircraft as a member of the international sales team of General Dynamics Corporation.

After retiring from the Marine Corps, LtCol Orson Swindle served as the Assistant Secretary of Commerce for Development. From 1997-2005, he was a commissioner on the U.S. Federal Trade Commission.

Lt Col Gene Smith became the airport manager for a large municipal airport and served as president and chairman of the board of the Air Force Association.

CAPT Everett Alvarez, USN, the POW who was captured first and held longest (eight and a half years), earned a master's degree and a JD degree. For several years he served as deputy director of the Peace Corps and deputy administrator of the Veterans Administration. He is founder and CEO of Alvarez and Associates, a thriving information technology company.

These are just a few from our group who came back home to lead with honor. In the POW camps they chose courage over compromise, commitment over comfort, and pain over shame. Their character, refined in the fires of captivity, propelled them to success in a wide range of endeavors.

The Key Leadership Ingredient

In this book we've talked about communication, teamwork, innovation, and other key leadership skills. Like blocking and tackling in football, mastery of these fundamentals is a prerequisite to leadership excellence. But these techniques, although essential, are not sufficient. They all must be undergirded by character.

Proverbs 11:3 says, "The integrity of the upright guides them, but the unfaithful are destroyed by their duplicity."[2] Your personal life matters. Harboring secrets and cutting corners compromises your moral authority and undermines your performance.

Authentic leaders consistently live in harmony with their values, even when no one is looking. Their walk matches their talk. They resist the temptation to achieve ends by less than honorable means. They are true to others, because they know they must be in order to be true to themselves.

Our nation desperately needs men and women who will lead with honor. They're needed in our businesses, our non-profit organizations, our governmental institutions, our families, our houses of worship, and in every other aspect of our society. Without such leaders, our society will decay and we will lose our freedom.

We also need men and women who will follow with honor by holding their leaders accountable to high standards. Our nation has made great strides toward tolerance in this country, but in the process I fear we have become far too tolerant of duplicitous leaders. Duplicity is almost an accepted practice in government, in the media, and in other areas of life. We have come to expect our leaders to "spin" their speech to suit the audience.

Recently a representative for a reputable polling organization said on a national TV news program that a candidate needed to change his views on a key position if he wanted to get elected. What? Is it now routinely assumed that leaders should jettison their established beliefs and commitments to gain position or wealth? Surely, this type of moral fluidity is not the path to individual and societal prosperity.

In the Introduction I said that if you want to lead with honor, you must become a warrior. You must be willing to engage in battles against your fears, your ingrained habits, and your natural instinct to put yourself first and take the easy way out. You must be willing to endure suffering and sacrifice for the sake of higher values.

Twenty-four hundred years ago the Greek historian Thucydides said, "The secret of happiness is freedom. And the secret of freedom is courage." The passage of time has not diminished the validity of his observation.

In this book I have introduced you to many courageous leaders who demonstrated unimaginable strength of character in situations of extreme vulnerability. I hope their stories have given you a new vision for the type of leader you want to be. And I hope the courage and perseverance they exhibited will inspire you to lean into your fears and break free from all hindrances that hold you back, so that you truly can lead with honor.

[1] *Stolen Valor: How the Vietnam Generation Was Robbed of Its Heroes and Its History,* B.G. Burkett and Glenna Whitley, Dallas: Verity Press, 1998.
[2] Proverbs 11:3 NIV

⑦ SUMMARY OF LESSONS: FOOT STOMPERS

Leadership is both simple and complex. When it gets complex, it's easy to hyper-focus on one problem, allowing the simple areas to drop off our radar. These are the times when I refer to my old notes and checklists to remind me of the important points of leadership. This summary of Foot Stompers is designed to be such an aid. I hope these lessons will serve you for a lifetime of leading with honor.

LEADING SELF

1. **Know Yourself.** Authentic leadership flows from the inside out. You will be most successful and fulfilled when you clarify who you uniquely are in terms of purpose, passion, and personality, and then lead authentically from that core.

2. **Guard Your Character.** Authentic leaders intentionally guard their character. Clarify your values with specificity and total honesty. Then structure a support team to help you live them with courage and transparency.

3. **Stay Positive.** A positive attitude is one of a leader's greatest assets, and it's one of the best ways you can influence/lead others. Keep your chin up, because when it goes down, you do too, and many others will follow right behind.

4. **Confront Your Doubts and Fears.** Authentic leaders develop courage as an act of will. Choose today to do what you know to be right, even when it feels unnatural or unsafe. Trust yourself, honor your values, lean into your pain, and intentionally engage issues with strength and humility, despite your fears.

5. **Fight to Win.** Successful leaders believe in their mission and fight to carry it out successfully. They don't quit; they expect to win; they take others with them; and they give others the credit.

6. **Bounce Back.** Authentic leaders know that life is difficult. They expect to get knocked down, and they have the proper attitude and outlook to enable them to persevere. You have a choice about how you will respond to difficulties. Confront the brutal realties of your situation, but never give up hope. Develop your plan, connect with your support team, and bounce back.

LEADING OTHERS

7. **Clarify and Build Your Culture.** Authentic leaders intentionally define and build cultures that further the mission, vision, and values of their organizations. Assess the culture of your organization and take the appropriate steps to make sure it is well defined, soundly structured, and effectively communicated.

8. **Over-Communicate the Message.** Effective communication requires intentional effort. To overcome the noise, distractions, and misinterpretations in the workplace, you must develop a clear message and a comprehensive communication plan. Then you must over-communicate your message multiple times through multiple channels.

9. **Develop Your People.** Authentic leaders engage in continual development. Knowledge alone is not enough; the only way to grow as a leader is to do things differently, and that requires change. Go first, and then take your people with you.

10. **Balance Mission and People.** Outstanding leaders balance accomplishment of the mission (results) and care for their people (relationships). However, the styles of most leaders are naturally biased toward one end of the spectrum or the other. To enhance your

leadership effectiveness, find out which types of skills you need to develop. Then, leaning into the pain of your doubts and fears, adapt your behaviors to do what you know a good leader should do.

11. **Build Cohesive Teams.** Build trust by helping teammates gain understanding, acceptance, and respect for each other. The resulting unity and cohesion will enable them to engage in creative conflict, which in turn will build the commitment and loyalty necessary to overcome the most difficult challenges.

12. **Exploit Creativity.** Think futuristically and innovate to stay competitive. Everyone has the capacity for innovative ideas; the leader's job is to draw them out. Harness the ideas of the creative folks, and allow them to pull you ahead of the competition.

13. **Treasure Your Trials and Celebrate Your Successes.** Effective leadership is forged in the crucible of struggles and fueled by the celebration of accomplishment. To promote teamwork and achieve success, treasure your trials and celebrate your victories.

14. **Free the Captives.** Authentic leaders proactively identify the shackles that hold them back and lean into the pain to break free and grow. As you gain your own freedom, begin helping others to do the same. Start by avoiding bitterness, connecting with your emotions, and doing the right thing even when it's difficult.

Appendix A: Map of North Vietnam Showing POW Camps

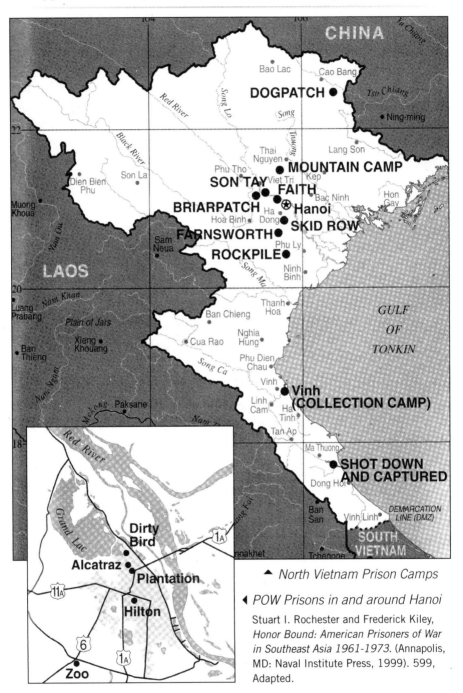

▲ North Vietnam Prison Camps

◀ POW Prisons in and around Hanoi

Stuart I. Rochester and Frederick Kiley, *Honor Bound: American Prisoners of War in Southeast Asia 1961-1973*. (Annapolis, MD: Naval Institute Press, 1999). 599, Adapted.

Appendix B: Military Code of Conduct

Military Code of Conduct

I

I am an American, fighting in the forces which guard my country and our way of life. I am prepared to give my life in their defense.

II

I will never surrender of my own free will. If in command, I will never surrender the members of my command while they still have the means to resist.

III

If I am captured, I will continue to resist by all means available. I will make every effort to escape and aid others to escape. I will accept neither parole nor special favors from the enemy.

IV

If I become a prisoner of war, I will keep faith with my fellow prisoners. I will give no information or take part in any action which might be harmful to my comrades. If I am senior, I will take command. If not, I will obey the lawful orders of those appointed over me, and will back them up in every way.

V

When questioned, should I become a prisoner of war, I am required to give only name, rank, service number, and date of birth. I will evade answering further questions to the utmost of my ability. I will make no oral or written statements disloyal to my country and its allies or harmful to their cause.

VI

I will never forget that I am an American, fighting for freedom, responsible for my actions, and dedicated to the principles which made my country free. I will trust in my God and in the United States of America.

Download your personal Honor Code at www.LeadingWithHonor.com/Book.

Appendix C: Camp Regulations (Feb 1967, Unedited)

In order to insure the proper execution of the regulations, the camp commander has decided to issue the following new regulations which have been modified and augmented to reflect the new conditions, from now on the criminals must strictly follow and abide by the following provisions:

The criminals are under an obligation to give full and clear written or oral answers to all questions raised by the camp authorities. All, attempts and tricks intended to evade answering further questions and acts directed to opposition by refusing to answer any questions will be considered manifestations of obstinacy and antagonism which deserves strict punishment.

The criminals must absolutely abide by and seriously obey all orders and instructions from Vietnamese officers and guards in the camp.

The criminals must demonstrate a cautious and polite attitude the officers and guards in the camp and must render greetings when met by them in a manner all ready determined by the camp authorities. When the Vietnamese Officers and Guards come to the rooms for inspection or when they are required by the camp officer to come to the room, the criminal must carefully and neatly put on their clothes, stand

attention, bow a greeting and await further orders. They may sit down only when permission is granted.

The criminal must maintain silence in the detention rooms and not make any loud noises which can be heard outside. All schemes and attempts to gain information and achieve communication with the criminals living next door by intentionally talking loudly, tapping on walls or by other means will be strictly punished.

If any criminal is allowed to ask a question he is allowed to say softly only the words "bao cao". The guard will report this to the officer in charge.

The criminals must go to bed and arise in accordance with the orders signaled by the gong.

When allowed outside for any reason each criminal is expected to walk only in the areas as limited by the guards-in-charge and seriously follow his instructions.

Any obstinacy or opposition, violation of the proceeding provisions, or any scheme or attempt to get out of the detention camp without permission are all punishable. On the other hand any criminal who strictly obeys the camp regulations and shows his true submission and repentance by his practical acts will be allowed to enjoy the humane treatment he deserves.

Anyone so imbued with a sense of preventing violations and who reveals the identity of those who attempt to act in violation of the forgoing provisions will be properly rewarded. However, if and criminal is aware of any violation and deliberately tries to cover it up, he will be strictly punished when this is discovered.

In order to assure the proper execution of the regulations, all the criminals in any detention room must be held responsible for any and all violations of the regulations committed in their room.

Signed
The Camp Commander

Appendix D: *Leadership Behavior DNA™* Assessment

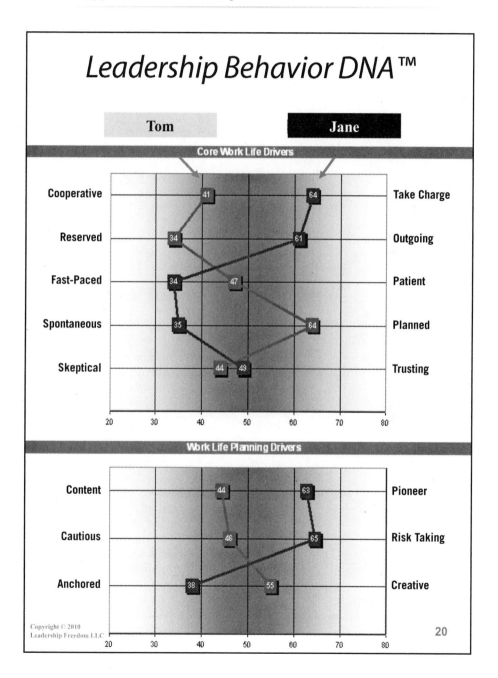

Appendix E: Emotions Chart

Joyful	Loved/Valued	Honored	Free	Hopeful	Useful	Confident
euphoric	accepted	admiration	alive	desire	achieving	bold
excited	adored	blessed	autonomy	dream	capable	brave
fulfilled	affection	credit	choices	eager	effective	challenged
glad	affirmed	fortunate	free	faith	open	daring
happy	approved	good	in control	optimism	powerful	determined
joy	cared for	honored	independent	trust	receptive	interested
joyous	content	important	open	encouraged	reliable	peaceful
jubilant	devotion	meaning	powerful	thankful	responsible	relaxed
pleased	intimacy	regarded	released	enthusiastic	satisfied	strong
pleasure	reassured	respect	unbound		useful	upbeat
positive	safe	special			worthwhile	content
relief	secure	tribute				awesome
delight	touched	unique				
delighted	trust					
elated	understood	**Neutral**				
cheerful	warmth	disinterested				
thrilled	ecstasy	reserved		**Surprise**		
ecstatic		flat		amazement		
		indifferent		shock		
				wonder		

Sadness	Shame/guilt	Anger	Disgust	Pain/Hurt	Fear	Angst
aching	ashamed	annoyed	aversion	affronted	afraid	anguish
agonized	awkward	antagonistic	contempt	disrespected	alarm	anxious
anguish	blamed	bitter	disgust	aching	anxiety	desperate
cynical	chagrin	end	distaste	hurt	anxious	panic
dejected	disgraced	enraged	repugnant	insulted	apprehensive	tension
depressed	dishonored	exasperated	revulsion	offended	doubtful	tormented
desolate	disrespected	furious	scorn	slighted	dread	worried
desolation	embarrassed	fury	scornful	snubbed	edgy	
despair	humiliated	hateful		upset	fearful	
despondent	remorse	hostile		wronged	frightened	
unhappy	worthless	irritated			nervous	
dismayed		resentful			panic	**Weak**
empathetic	**Disappointment**		**Confusion**	**Lonely**	scared	dependent
gloom	betrayed		hesitant	alienated	tense	deprived
grief	crushed		indecisive	alone	terrified	feeble
heartbroken	disillusioned		skeptical	ostracized	terror	helpless
hopeless	frustrated		uncertain	rejected	wary	impotent
lonely				useless		needy
self-pity				distant		paralyzed
sorrowful				dull		powerless
sympathetic				shutdown		vulnerable
withdrawn						weary

Appendix F: Military Rank Abbreviations

MILITARY RANK ABBREVIATIONS						
PAY GRADE	**ARMY**	**MARINE CORPS**	**NAVY**	**AIR FORCE**	**COAST GUARD**	**CIVILIAN**
Enlisted						
E-1	PV1	Pvt	SR	AB	SR	
E-2	PV2	Pfc	SA	Amn	SA	
E-3	PFC	LCpl	SN	A1C	SN	
E-4	SPC	Cpl	P03	SrA	P03	
E-5	SGT	Sgt	P02	SSgt	P02	
E-6	SSG	SSgt	P01	TSgt	P01	
E-7	SFC	GySgt	CPO	MSgt	CPO	
E-8	MSG 1SG	MSgt 1stSgt	SCPO	SMSgt	SCPO	
E-9	SGM CSM	MGySgt SgtMaj	MCPO	CMSgt	MCPO	
Service Senior Enlisted Advisors	SMA	SMMC	MCPON	CMSAF	MCPO-CG	
Warrant Officers						
W-1	WO1	WO	--	--	--	
W-2	CW2	CWO2	CWO2	--	CWO2	
W-3	CW3	CWO3	CWO3	--	CWO3	
W-4	CW4	CWO4	CWO4	--	CWO4	
W-5	CW5	CWO5	CWO5	--	--	
Officer						
0-1	2LT	2ndLt	ENS	2d Lt	ENS	GS-7 GS-8
0-2	1LT	1stLt	LTJG	1st Lt	LTJG	GS-9
0-3	CPT	Capt	LT	Capt	LT	GS-10 GS-11
0-4	MAJ	Maj	LCDR	Maj	LCDR	GS-12
0-5	LTC	LtCol	CDR	Lt Col	CDR	GS-13 GS-14
0-6	COL	Col	CAPT	Col	CAPT	GS-15
0-7	BG	BGen	RDML	Brig Gen	RDML	SES
0-8	MG	MajGen	RADM	Maj Gen	RADM	SES
0-9	LTG	LtGen	VADM	Lt Gen	VADM	SES
0-10	GEN	Gen	ADM	Gen	ADM	

Note: The above chart is intended to display the military rank abbreviations. The civilian equivalence is included as a general comparison and is NOT intended to establish precedence. SES precedence for civilian employees is based on position and not pay grade.

ACKNOWLEDGEMENTS

When my fellow POWs and I walked out of that prison in North Vietnam, we were overwhelmed with gratitude for the many who had worked and prayed for our safe release. That sense of gratitude has remained with me every day since, and I want to take this opportunity to thank a few of the people who have made significant contributions to my life and, directly or indirectly, to this book.

My heartfelt appreciation goes out to
- Our fellow warriors, who were willing to do anything to get us out.
- Our national leaders, who made sure we did get out.
- The National League of POW/MIA Families, who worked so hard to improve our lot and gain a full accounting of our status.
- Ross Perot and his team of EDS and Dallas folks, who did so much to support our families and us during and after the war.
- Maxine McCaffrey, dear friend and talented artist, who took up our cause and touched the hearts of so many Americans with her extraordinary artwork. Her exceptional art is on display in the POW Alcove near E-ring in the Pentagon.
- Dr. Roger Shields, former Assistant Secretary of Defense for POW/MIA Affairs, who managed Operation Homecoming.
- The many POW/MIA bracelet wearers around the country who made sure we were not forgotten.

Turning homeward, I want to acknowledge the sacrifices made by my family, whose unfailing love and support meant so much. My parents, Molene and Leon, are gone now, but they soldiered for our cause and prayed like warriors. They led with honor, and they taught me about honor. That made all the difference, and I honor them for the lives they lived.

To my brother, Robert, and my sister-in-law, Pat, I've never been able to thank you adequately for what you did for me during those difficult years. I can only imagine what you went through. Thank you for your faithfulness, then and now.

Thank you to my extended family and friends in Commerce, Nicholson, and Athens, Georgia, and in Jackson and Madison counties. I'll single out my dear friend Sally Tucker, as representative of so many of you who stood by me, not only in your thoughts and prayers, but also by your actions to raise awareness of my plight.

Writing this book has been much more difficult than I expected. It required a tremendous amount of emotional energy to revisit the details of my POW experience, and I could not have completed this project without the support of many people.

I had not met my wonderful wife, Mary, before I went off to war, so thankfully she missed that experience. But she deserves sainthood for her patience and forbearance with me as I labored for two years in my "war with words"—close to a hundred thousand, if you count all the edits and deletions. She has never been a golf widow, but she knows what it's like to spend evenings and weekends alone, and she has handled it well. She also has labored to read and edit with her eagle eye, providing objective feedback as my co-laborer to help shape this book. Thanks, Dear, for all your love and support.

My kids have all contributed in their own special ways through both good ideas and encouragement. Thanks Pat, Kristy, Lance, and Meredith. Likewise, Barbara Owens, our dear friend, who has championed this work for a long time.

I don't think I would have ever reached the finish line without the help of my talented editor Michael Dowling (http://www.MichaelJ-Dowling.com). He's a good man with words, and when I ran out of energy or expressions, Mike saddled up as my ghostwriter. Mike's been a joy to work with; he totally dedicated himself to this project.

As we were finishing the writing, Kevin Light came alongside to manage the production and marketing of the book. He knew how to get a book through the many steps to make it to the shelves. Publishing coach Rob Eager helped me refine the message and develop my first book proposal. Leadership consultant Debbie Shine stepped in to enhance the online coaching. I'll always be grateful to these professionals.

I have drawn strength from family and so many friends during this endeavor. People far and near—some who hardly know me—have provided ideas and encouragement. Their support reminds me of my experience running the Atlanta Peachtree 10K race, when cheering fans lining the streets urged the other runners and me onward. At one point, as I was straining up the long and appropriately named Cardiac Hill, a band began playing upbeat music that lifted my spirits and gave me the necessary energy to mount that dreaded incline. Your fellowship has provided the same type of inspiration to me throughout this long writing journey.

Knowing I won't remember all who need to be singled out, I muster the courage to name a few:

- Hugh Massie has been a great asset as a loyal friend and a strategic partner dedicated to leading with honor.
- Larry Bolden has been a great friend and coach, helping me to clarify my commitments and the purpose of this book. The staff and board at Wellspring Group have encouraged me at every turn.
- My support team of John Purcell and Dan Brown provided weekly encouragement, always affirming my ideas and talents.
- Dick Bruso has been an encourager and advisor for many years and his insights on the book were always helpful.
- Jack Hodge's confidence in me and his belief in this book have been monumental. Likewise have been the longtime mentoring and special friendship of Don Jacobsen.
- Maj Gen George "Nordie" Norwood and Todd Tibbetts have gently and regularly pushed me along to just "get it done."
- Friends at CEO Netweavers who have cheered me onward.
- My leadership-consulting friends Greg Hiebert, Craig Jones, Gary O'Malley, and Rob Ketterer provided ideas and great feedback at key points to help me hone the message.

- Of course, I'm very grateful for the privilege of working with great clients over the years. These leaders have provided the experiences that I share in this book. In the process of serving them, they've taught me so much.

Many former POW friends have contributed to this effort by clarifying details and reminding me of stories. Thanks to each of you for your time and patience. Mike McGrath, former president of Nam-Pow, and our all-time historian, has been a huge supporter. He generously shared his repository of "Mac's Facts," and in cooperation with Naval Institute Press, he allowed me to publish five of his lifelike sketches of POW life.

I've been overwhelmed by the kind words of so many who have taken the time to review this book and endorse it. My heartfelt thanks goes out to each of you for putting your stamp of approval on this book for others to see.

With so many providing encouragement and support, I'm sure that I have overlooked someone. Please forgive me and grant me grace.

My desire and mission has always been to honor God: Father, Son, and Holy Spirit. The Trinity has kept me, loved me, and given me the gift of faith to believe, in good times and bad. I have truly been lifted up by eagles' wings. Thank you, Lord.

Throughout history, nations and peoples around the world have established monuments to great battles. In ancient times the memorial was often a stone or a pile of rocks. In 1 Samuel 7:12, to recognize God's help in winning a comeback battle, Samuel erects a stone and calls it Ebenezer, which means "stone of help."

Truly, God was with my fellow POWs and me during our battle, and I hope this book will be an Ebenezer to recognize and honor His power and His faithfulness.

INDEX

ABOUT THE AUTHOR

Lee Ellis

Lee Ellis is President and Founder of Leadership Freedom® LLC and FreedomStar Media.™ For more than twenty years he has served as an executive coach, leadership consultant, and Certified Speaking Professional (CSP) in the areas of leadership, teambuilding, and human performance. His past clients include Fortune 500 senior executives and C-Level leaders in telecommunications, healthcare, military, and other business sectors. His speaking and media appearances include interviews on networks such as CNN, CBS This Morning, C-Span, ABC World News, Fox News Channel, plus hundreds of speaking engagements in various industry sectors throughout the world.

Early in his career, Lee's interest in leadership was piqued when he served as an Air Force fighter pilot flying fifty-three combat missions over North Vietnam. In 1967, he was shot down and held as a POW for more than five years in Hanoi and surrounding camps. After the war he served as an instructor pilot, chief of flight standardization/evaluation, and flying squadron commander. Additionally he commanded two leadership development organizations before retiring as a colonel. Lee's combat decorations include two Silver Stars, the Legion of Merit, the Bronze Star with Valor device, the Purple Heart, the Air Medal with eight Oak Leaf Clusters, and the POW medal.

Lee has a BA in History and a MS in Counseling and Human Development. He is a graduate of the Armed Forces Staff College and the Air War College. Lee has authored or co-authored five books on leadership and career development.

He and his wife Mary reside in Atlanta, GA and have four grown children and six grandchildren.

TAKE THE NEXT STEP IN
YOUR LEADERSHIP JOURNEY

A FREE Leadership Discovery Report for *Leading with Honor* Readers

The first lesson in *Leading with Honor* is entitled "know yourself."

Before executing decisions in leadership and leading others, the foundational step in leadership is knowing who you are—your strengths and struggles that uniquely position you for fulfillment and success in life and work.

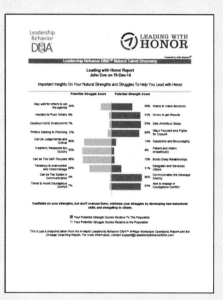

Take 10 minutes to complete the FREE *Leading with Honor* Discovery Report to get an instant snapshot of where you are today as a leader. Register now at LeadingWithHonor.com/Talent.

Then, we'll give you the opportunity to explore your unique leadership style more in-depth with our *Leadership Behavior DNA™* Assessment and coaching options.

At **LeadingWithHonor.com**, FREE materials are available to dig deeper into the lessons provided in *Leading with Honor* –

- Read helpful articles that you can use for personal study or with your team.

- Download more Coaching materials to help you or your team apply *Leading with Honor* lessons.

- View more photos of Lee's POW experience.